Peanut Butter on the Wall & Marshmallows in the Microwave

Margaret LisaHanna
What is your story?
3/18

Peanut Butter on the Wall & Marshmallows in the Microwave

Memories of Raising Six Hannas in Gahanna

Margaret Leis Hanna

Book Design & Production
Columbus Publishing Lab
www.ColumbusPublishingLab.com

Print ISBN: 978-1-63337-180-4
E-book ISBN: 978-1-63337-179-8

Printed in the United States of America
1 3 5 7 9 10 8 6 4 2

To David and Rosie

INTRODUCTION

"How did you manage a household of eight?

How did you cope with six personalities?

How did you travel with so many children?"

My husband Bill and I looked at each other on many occasions and prayed for guidance as we, two only children, raised six Hannas in Gahanna.

We coped the best we could. Prayer, love, humor, anger, fear and friends helped us become a strong family.

I write about our experiences in a slice of Americana starting in 1969.

Everyday happenings occurred in our household of teens and curfews, tots and time-outs, calm and chaos. Some are humorous. Some are sad. Some are hair-raising. All are true.

In 1970 we bought a house in Gahanna, Ohio, a suburb of Columbus, Ohio. With five boys and one girl, we outgrew it. In 1987 we bought a bigger house in the same town.

Peanut butter on the wall and marshmallows in the microwave are two scenes from the ever-changing Hanna household of eight.

Walk through the rooms of the two houses with me and discover flying plates, flying babies and a flying angel. Travel cross country with us. Enter our unfamiliar emotional territory as we hang onto each other.

Each chapter/room reveals stories of raising six children of all ages and stages together. If you are raising or have raised a large family, grew up in a large family, know a large family, or are curious about a large family, you can relate to some of the happenings, recall similar situations and realize these scenes occur in any era, any size family with someone saying, "I didn't do it! STOP IT!" or "My turn…"

Enjoy your tour of this mother's memories, interspersed with reflections created in those moments as I change and mature with my children.

Part I
Heil Drive Hanna House

ONE

If you can say banana...you can say Gahanna

—A T-shirt printed in the 1970s

"Your name is what?" I was ordering an item from a catalog by phone.

"And you live where?" I heard the person on the other end snicker.

"Let me get this straight," the male voice said. "Your name is Mrs. Hanna."

I nodded as if he could see me.

"And you live in Gahanna." More snickers. "On Heil Drive?" an outright guffaw.

"Are you kidding me? Mrs. Hanna from Gahanna?"

"No, I am not," I said in my schoolteacher voice.

Friends chided us, too. "You've got a lot of nerve. Who would want to be Hannas on Heil in Gahanna?"

Bill and I did.

On our way to becoming the Hannas of Gahanna, we came from Cleveland, Ohio. Bill had accepted a job in Columbus, the state capital. We were advised to live on the east side of the city near the airport as his job required traveling.

Bill and I and our toddler son Lee came to Columbus in August 1969 and rented a townhouse on the southeast side of the city.

We found a two-floor, three-bedroom townhouse with a full basement in Reynoldsburg, Ohio, fifteen miles east of Columbus. We moved into an end unit of Williamsburg Square, a newly built Colonial structure, as its first renters.

The first floor had an open plan with living room, dining area and kitchen with a new Harvest Gold refrigerator, stove and dishwasher. Lee had graduated from a feeding table to a "youth chair" and was proud to sit at the table with us.

One of Lee's favorite toys, the Fisher-Price barn and animals, sat under the table. The barn door "mooed" whenever opened. As Lee carried the barn around the house, his opening and closing the door let me know where he was.

He and I watched the first *Sesame Street* in November 1969. At seventeen months, Lee sat on my lap and clapped as he pointed to the screen, entranced by Big Bird, Oscar the Grouch and Cookie Monster. I knew we'd make time to watch the program every day. It aired out of Pittsburgh featuring personalities I recognized from my Pittsburgh days. The show made me homesick.

Upstairs were three bedrooms, a bath, master, a small bedroom for Lee and a guest room waiting for grandparents' visits.

The half-finished basement held Bill's newly-built workbench and reconstructed platform for his hobby of model railroading. Above the workbench hung a rack with Lee's first-year baby food jars filled with nuts and bolts. Lee played in a big box next to the workbench. It had held parts for Bill's current project, which we eagerly awaited. He built a Heathkit color TV.

After nine months in the town house, we were ready to look for a "real" house. The 270 bypass around Columbus was being built behind us.

Another friend told us to buy a house on the east side of Columbus. "Bill won't have to drive to work into sunrise or home from work into sunset." We never thought of that situation. We followed the advice and found a two-story house on Heil Drive in Gahanna, ten minutes from the airport.

Bill and I grew up in two-story homes. We liked the privacy of upstairs bedrooms and wanted a full basement for his model railroad. In our own functional but not fancy house, Bill and I, five sons and a daughter became the noisy, happy household of Hannas from Gahanna.

The boys learned to answer the phone as "Hanna House number (position in family) speaking," or "Hanna House (name) speaking."

We were constantly asked, "Are you related to Jack Hanna?" He was the Columbus Zoo director in 1969. Although we met him soon after we arrived, we learned that his family was from Kentucky and ours from Pennsylvania.

Lee knew he belonged in our new town. We pulled into the parking lot of the local hardware store. "Look," Lee yelled, pointing to the garage behind the store.

"Where?" I asked.

He pointed to two signs, one on each side of the garage door. One sign advertised Lee jeans, the other, Hanna paints. "Lee Hanna, that's me!"

Having a rhyming name did help. Mrs. Hanna from Gahanna is hard to forget. The last name Hanna limited us when naming a girl. We didn't want a name that ended with "a", although Bill's grandmother was Anna Hanna. I would have liked to name our daughter Mary Margaret as a good Catholic family name and call her Molly. Our boys talked us out of that name. "Molly Hanna sounds too much like Pollyanna," they said. "We don't want the label of a do-gooder pinned on her."

As only children, having more than one child was important to us. We never thought we'd be blessed with six children! Our oldest and youngest are sixteen years apart. We have been parenting for almost fifty years! I could wear the T-shirt that reads "I'm a mother. I'm not afraid of anything!"

"I never cut grass," Bill says, watches people's expression, grins and continues, "I don't need to. I have five boys." We've dealt with many problems with the diversity of personalities and activities in our family. Lee and Greg's personalities were so different that we thought Jay's would be in between. His was unique as were all the other children's!

In a 1978 letter from my mother, who raised only one, she writes, "How do you and Bill remember three personalities?" She did not live to know the personalities of her six grandchildren. We have two librarians, a government analyst, an electrician, an actor, and a doctor. With each child, I became more accepting of differences in people.

Our first son, Lee, is William Leis. Leis is my maiden name. When I was pregnant with him, my mother-in-law told me that the first male in the family should be named William plus the mother's maiden name. I felt duly charged to carry on the tradition. Bill is William Thompson Hanna, his mother's maiden name. We didn't want a Billy, so we started calling our first son Lee, a shortened version of my maiden name. Lee has grown up to be the serious one, with a dry sense of humor like his father, the one who takes care of others. He taught us how to be parents. We saw him as innocently honest.

When the tooth fairy visited for the first time and left a quarter, Lee handed the coin back to us saying, "Here, I already have one."

When Lee married, I made the same statement about the family name that Bill's mother gave me. His first son is William Swan Hanna, another William with his mother's maiden name.

Our second son, Gregory Michael, is my dad in a skinny body. He can talk to anyone about anything! He's also funny.

In a letter from Bill's mother she reminded us of my comment that Greg, a toddler at the time, walked up to a fire hydrant, put his hat on it and talked to it as if it were the natural thing to do.

In his older years, Greg delighted in telling all, "Mom and Pop were married on August first. I was born on August eighth." He omitted the six years in between!

I often wondered if my mother's maiden name "Craig" influenced me to name him Greg. We were pleased that he and his wife also carried on a family name. They named their daughter Ruth, Bill's mother's name and my middle name. We felt free from using a family name for Greg as we included both families in Lee's name. I loved the combination of Gregory Alan. We couldn't give him that name and set him up for a lifetime of teasing. Greg would have been G.A. Hanna living in Gahanna.

Our third son, Jay Robert, was named for the blue jays in our yard and our friend Bob. Robert is the patron saint of librarians. Jay is a librarian. Who knew he would follow the profession? He is also an instructor of Krav Maga, a self-protection program. Jay is the compassionate one with a lot of courage.

He told us, "I don't think I can hack it at St. Charles." (The Catholic preparatory high school where Lee and Greg graduated.) "I'm not the student they are."

Bill and I agreed. We didn't want to put the pressure on him in a prep school. Jay did well at Gahanna Lincoln High School, the local public high school. He had the courage to spend a school year in Germany as an exchange student between high school and college. He took two planes and three trains to get to his host home on the coast of the Baltic Sea. His keen sense of humor surprises us. He keeps his cell phone in his pocket and sometimes says, "Excuse me. My pants are ringing."

Our fourth son, Stephen Richard, is our actor. He plays many roles on and off stage. His flair for the dramatic surfaced early. One Halloween, he was five and sick. He couldn't go out trick-or-treating. He sat inside on the steps and loudly announced to all who came to our door, "This is the worst night of my life!" Stephen is a host and waiter at Spaghetti Warehouse, Uncle Silly to the nieces and nephews, the family events planner and a charmer. He is happiest when he's on stage. With his deep voice and inflections, he sounds and looks like Jeremy Irons.

Our daughter, Kristin Marie, was the first girl in the Hanna family in seventy-five years. After naming four boys, we gave the boys three acceptable combinations of names for a girl. I was excited to have a girl in the family for girly things. I could dress her in pink frilly dresses, have tea parties and play with dolls.

It took time for the family to get used to having a girl in the house. "Does she wake up talking?" the boys asked. "Why does she cry so easily?"

One evening Bill was reprimanding the teenage boys, and turned around and spoke to three-year-old Kristin in the same angry voice. She wet her pants. Bill learned that he couldn't speak to her in the same tone.

With five brothers, Kristin learned to hold her own and speak her mind. When she entered middle school, she declared, "No more pink! From now on my color is purple!"

Our fifth son, Roy Austin, was named for his grandfathers: Roy Hanna and Austin Leis. The older boys chose his name also. Bill's father had died by this time, but he knew the Hanna name was carried on in his first three grandsons. My dad was proud to know his name was continued. It took Bill a long time getting used to calling his son by his father's name.

Roy is our Eagle Scout, Marine and athlete. When he went for his wrestling physical our family doctor asked him why he chose that sport. "You're going to be thrown all over the place," he said. "Why would you want that?"

"Why not," Roy answered. "I'm used to it. My brothers throw me around all the time."

With the sixteen-year difference in ages, I thought Lee and Roy might not know each other but, when we took toddler Roy to visit Lee in college, Lee was glad to show him around his dorm. Roy was the hit of the day.

Bill is a retired engineer/research scientist. I am a former teacher. We met the summer of 1960 when our parents were vacationing at Edinboro Lake north of Pittsburgh, Pennsylvania. Our dads were golfers and the area was known for its good golf courses. Bill was in summer school at Carnegie Institute of Technology in Pittsburgh. I was working college summers as a waitress at Chautauqua Lake in New York. We came to visit our parents on the same weekend. Our parents knew each other in our hometown of Aliquippa, Pennsylvania. Bill and his mother stopped at my parents' cottage to say hello.

I had just got up on a Saturday morning. Wrapped in a blanket, with my hair sticking straight up, I looked like a walking teepee. I shuffled out from my bedroom to face Bill and his mom.

Ours was not love at first sight, but Bill did say, "My parents come here every summer. I can show you around the area later, if you'd like." I gave him a sleepy nod and went back to bed.

We spent that evening together and talked easily about everything. That fall Bill traveled to Grove City College—where I was a junior—to attend a Grove City/Carnegie Tech football game. I was at my standing Saturday babysitting job for a professor's children and didn't attend the game. I didn't know Bill was on campus. When I learned about this trip years later, I felt terrible that we missed each other. Our relationship resumed New Year's Eve. We were back in our hometown for winter break. "Let's meet to welcome in 1961" started our dating years.

Even on their death beds, our parents wouldn't admit they set us up! They had known each other for many years. Bill's aunt was my dad's secretary at the bank. Bill's mother was in my aunt's bridge club.

Bill and I went to the same high school and church and never met. I knew his name since he was a junior taking senior classes. I knew he won many science awards in high school. I doubt that he even knew about me. We went on to separate colleges. I graduated from Aliquippa High School in 1958 and Bill in 1959.

I graduated from Grove City College in 1962, with a Bachelor of Arts degree in Elementary Education and a minor in French. That summer I started graduate classes in education at University of Pittsburgh focusing on teaching reading. In the fall, I began teaching first grade, then reading and French in junior high. I continued attending summer classes at Pitt. It seemed to me that the Grove City College campus could fit in any one of its buildings. I learned to navigate its campus spread over one section of the city. I was also in classes with people who had taught for years and felt the competition. Going there was overwhelming. I did what my mother always told me, "Act like you know what you're doing."

Bill graduated from Carnegie Institute of Technology in 1963 with a Bachelor of Science degree in Mechanical Engineering and continued there in graduate school. We were married August 1, 1964. He claims we were married on the first of the month "so I can remember the date!"

We were happy to face our years of graduate school together in a tiny apartment in Sewickley, Pennsylvania, halfway between our schools. Bill was in ROTC and received extensions for graduate school. He graduated in 1965 with a Master of Science degree in Electrical Engineering as an officer in the US Army. I continued teaching until he graduated in 1967 with a PhD in Mechanical Engineering.

At graduation, Bill was assigned to the Ordnance Officer's Orientation Course at Aberdeen Proving Grounds, Maryland. We rented a summer home off base with another couple, Patty and Gus. Bill and Gus had met in the engineering program at Carnegie Tech and Patty and I became friends.

Gus and Patty taught us to love California wines. We taught them how to bake pies. No "meet pies" was Bill's request. "Meet pies don't hold enough filling when the top and bottom crusts meet," he stated. I filled pies with double ingredients, so "top and bottom crusts wouldn't meet."

It was hard for Patty and me to conform to army regulations for officers' wives. "You will smile. You will wear white gloves. You will have a good time" seemed to be our motto. We were always afraid our actions might cause our husbands to be demoted. Bill and Gus graduated with National Aeronautics and Space Administration/NASA assignments—Gus to California and Bill to Ohio. We had been married three years. I had worked in my career and was ready to be a stay-at-home mom. That summer, I became pregnant.

We were going to be parents. We were excited and proud to go back home between assignments and tell our parents they were to be grandparents. We drove from eastern Maryland to western Pennsylvania, stopping at almost every gas station. The trip took longer than it should have because I was constantly saying, "We have to stop at the next gas station!"

Bill would sigh and say, "But we don't need gas!"

I'd squirm in my seat and say, "But I have to pee!"

We spent a year in Cleveland, Ohio while Bill completed his military assignment at NASA Lewis Space Center, now NASA Glenn—named for Ohio's astronaut John Glenn. Military families welcomed us and acquainted us with the area. We were happy to be included. I asked the older sister of my childhood friend Lynn for advice. Mary Claire lived in the area and recommended an obstetrician and a dentist and helped me sew maternity clothes.

Bill and I lived off base as civilians since there was no army base nearby. While Bill was at work in the labs, I savored time alone with no classes to prepare, no schedule to follow, no drive to work. I was blessed with an easy pregnancy and was able to walk to the local library branch and read books I never had time to read.

My dad drove my mother out to help me at the baby's due date. I was so big I didn't think my skin could stretch more. When my dad saw me he laughed and said, "You look like you swallowed a watermelon." I was hurt. I was more than ready to have my first child, but I didn't laugh. My dad returned home and my mother waited with us for a week after the due date and had to return home. It was comforting to have my mother there, although frustrating that she had to leave.

Lee was born at Fairview General Hospital in Cleveland on April 9,1968. Bill and I drove to the hospital at 6:30 a.m. on a Tuesday morning. Labor was induced a few hours later. In the labor room, I was over excited and started throwing up, so I was sedated and Bill was sent home. I slept all day and woke up just in time to see my baby born at 8:15 that evening. I was a mother!

Bill was called in and we admired our child together. We couldn't believe we had produced this beautiful eight-and-a-half-pound baby. Since Bill was on active duty, with no military hospital nearby, Lee was born in a civilian hospital. Bill loves to tell all, "My son was a Medicare baby!" (The medical insurance the service offered for off base servicemen.) Lee cost us only the price of the phone in my room.

Bill's mother waited in Pennsylvania until Lee was born. His dad brought her to stay with us and to see his first grandson. I loved the help. I didn't realize how tiring keeping house and tending a newborn could be. I'm an organized person and was sure I could handle everything when she left. Bill and I were both sleep deprived by the end of the next week. That condition lasted throughout the year as I nursed this baby who seemed hungry every two hours. My constant cry was, "I need time to do more than nurse a baby!"

Both sets of parents traveled to Cleveland when Lee was baptized four weeks later. He wore the long white embroidered baptismal gown Bill wore twenty-six years before. We were carrying on another Hanna tradition.

Lee was born with red hair. I was a brunette and Bill a blond. My dad teased again. "He must have gotten the red hair from the milkman!"

I could laugh at this comment and respond, "Our milkman is bald!"

Bill's army assignment was ending. He spent the summer interviewing for a job. Lee must have thought Sunday evenings were "airport time." He would sit in his stroller and wave "goodbye" to Pop as Bill went off for another interview. Lee pointed to things and called them "da," but Bill was always "Pop." Bill came home Monday nights or Tuesday mornings and we waited for letters and phone calls for further interviews or letters of acceptance from companies in several states. I was ready to take our little family anywhere.

I traveled with Bill for an interview in California. We renewed our friendship with Patty and Gus who showed us sights along the West Coast. We also flew to Hawaii where my childhood friend Joyce and her husband lived. We visited with them for a week and enjoyed the spectacular views of the islands.

Our mothers looked after one-year-old Lee in Cleveland. It was tiring for each of them to watch their first grandchild. As our first time away as parents, we called home several times. "How's Lee doing without us?"

"He's fine," our mothers said, but we could hear the tiredness in their voices. It was freeing to travel as a couple again. I loved the time away to be a relaxed wife and not a tired mommy.

We returned to receive a letter requesting an interview for Bill in Columbus, Ohio. A job offer followed.

We moved to Columbus and Bill began his thirty-four-year career at Battelle Memorial Institute; a not-for-profit research center. The city wasn't as sophisticated as Pittsburgh or Cleveland, and one day I called Bill at work and asked, "What kind of place did you bring me to? I just heard on TV that cows were on the freeway!" A part of that freeway (I-270 outer belt) was being built behind us beyond our miniscule patio and tall privacy fence. The twenty-four-hour noise of the machines and nighttime bright lights shining into our town house prompted us to move. We knew we wanted more than one child and were ready for a bigger family and a bigger house. We were happy to learn that I was pregnant again.

The three of us moved into Gahanna and the Heil Drive house the spring of 1970. It was exciting to move into our own place and begin our life as a bigger family.

The realtor asked why my hand shook when I signed the mortgage. "I never thought of living in 2000," I said.

After six years of renting, we were finally homeowners. We were responsible for a mortgage and upkeep of a house larger than anything we had rented. I was comfortable with the location. As a former teacher, I had researched school districts on the east side of Columbus. I liked the curriculum I saw in Gahanna. I believed our children could receive a good education. The elementary school was within walking distance, the middle school and high school were within bike-riding distance.

Friends asked, "Why do you want a four-bedroom house with only one child?"

In the succeeding years, we filled the four bedrooms and more.

Named

At Baptism, name received
Not known when conceived.
Four ancestors carried the same
From mother's family they came.

In Childhood I would come
To the nickname of the formal one
In school years family and friends
Knew me by the name I penned.

Changes came, new names to add
Confirmation, college, Miss added as a grad
Name no longer from father and mother
But married name from another.

Now naming as a mother
My turn to name another
My maiden name, two grandfathers'
Only one, a daughter's.

For a grandchild given my name,
An honor of unprecedented gain
I am happy to lend.
Knowing the name will never end.

Forgetting names now my lot.
"Tell me your name. I forgot."
I say too often in recent days
In my head too many names at play.

I am named
Peggy Leis / Margaret Ruth Leis
Peg Hanna / Margaret Leis Hanna
But the best names are

Dear
     Mom
          Grandma

CHAPTER
TWO

Where?

"Oh, I know that house," Jerry the barber said when I took Lee for his first Gahanna haircut. Jerry laughed. "It's sitting on the swamp where I used to catch frogs when I was a boy!"

When I mentioned our address to others who were from the area, they verified his story. "Your house WAS built on an underground spring!"

Then I worried. What had we bought?

I couldn't imagine how an old swamp could affect us in 1970. The house was six years old when we bought it and still standing. I quickly learned the effects of the swamp and the use of a sump pump.

Bill and I had never heard of a sump pump. It was not needed in the hills of Pennsylvania. We quickly learned its value in flat Ohio. Our pump ran constantly.

One winter night Bill and I came home from a company function and didn't hear the familiar hum of the pump. Bill started down the steps to the basement. "Oh shit," he yelled.

I peered over his shoulder to find the basement floor flooded. The sump pump had stopped running. Kicking off his shoes, Bill threw off his suit jacket, loosened his tie, rolled up his pant legs, grabbed a broom and began sweeping water toward the drain. I kicked off my shoes, pulled off my hose, hiked up my skirt and grabbed a mop.

For hours, we sloshed around in two to three inches of fast gushing water. As fast as we could, we pushed it toward the floor drain. The line taking water outside had frozen and the pump couldn't pump water out! We finally realized that all we could do was let the water flow toward the drain, and go to bed. We were exhausted. As I drifted off to sleep, I wondered what other new experiences our house might bring.

The following spring, Bill dug the line out into the street and rebuilt it with new pipes. The old pipes had cracked and water was surfacing into the yard. Inside, he built shelves under the basement steps, raising them a few feet above the floor to save items stored there from future floods.

Bill had collected years of railroad magazines from which he would combine plans and build a railroad in our basement. He had to throw out the soggy magazines stored on the low shelves, disappointed at the loss of information.

Bill calculated how much water pumped out of our ground each day, and always the engineer, declared, "Look at the amount of water running down the street! I could build an irrigation system for the front yard from the water pumped out of our basement." I believed him.

In the front yard, near where the pipes were replaced, we planted a plum tree.

Later, when Kristin was born, friends decorated our plum tree with pink crepe paper and placed a huge pink sign on the garage door. We were proud to let the world know about a Hanna girl. After years of suspecting neighbors of decorating our house, I was shocked to find others were the culprits. I was embarrassed to have accused the wrong people, but happy to know others cared about our family. I stammered an apology to the wrongly accused.

Adding more color to the beige stucco, we painted our shutters the rust color in the brick lining the face of the house. An attached two-car garage sat to the east, the door painted rust with white accent. A long front porch with six white columns supported the porch roof. Bill always wanted to build a railing between them, sentimentalizing, "So I can sit with my feet propped up and watch thunderstorms like I did back home with my dad." I liked the porch lined with shrubs.

In the corner of the porch sat an old milk can spray painted to match the rust trim. Often Lee would sit on the antique can reading a book. To be sent outside to play was punishment for him. He would take a book and read, either on that milk can or high up in the backyard maple tree where he couldn't be seen. Years later I learned that with all his allergies, he was miserable being outside! He was punished physically (asthma) and isolated for what he'd done. I felt like a wicked witch who had cast a double spell on my son.

In the backyard Bill built a multi-colored playhouse, which started out as a free-standing platform with a ladder and railing painted primary colors. Later a roof was added and a sandbox was dug under the playhouse. Many children's plays were enacted from above. Actors appeared from behind sheets suspended from the roof.

Its deck was also a fishing pier. The boys fished for metal jar lids strewn around the yard. I read about this game in a magazine. Using a stick, a string and a magnet the boys caught and re-caught their "fish." I could clean house in peace and glance out the window to watch them "fishing."

The deck also became the bridge of a pirate ship and I would hear "Ships ahoy." As a lighthouse, its rotating beacon was a boy with a flashlight. As a conning tower of a submarine, its searches were called out by boys using empty paper towel rolls as binoculars.

Half the backyard was a twenty-foot terraced hill. At the foot of the hill, we planted a garden. Squirrels loved our produce. Bill claimed they thumbed their noses at us! We had to fence in the area from animals and humans. High school kids crossed the open field above and used our hillside as a shortcut to Heil Drive. "This is not your yard," I'd yell in my schoolteacher voice. "You're scaring our kids playing here and ruining our garden." My scolding was ineffective. We installed a six-foot fence.

One Friday night after a high school football game, as Bill and I were lying in bed, we heard screams from the backyard. Three teens ran down the hill toward the chicken wire fence gleaming in the moonlight. The first guy saw the fence. "A fence," he yelled as he jumped in time to clear it.

The second ran into the fence post, knocked it over and ripped out a portion of the fence. "Man, I ripped my jacket," he yelled as he tumbled into the yard.

We watched the shortest stumble and fall flat on the chicken wire and give a blood-curdling scream. "It got my balls," he wailed. His friends picked him up and helped him limp through the yard toward Heil Drive.

We heard, "This isn't worth it!"

The word got around about our "killer fence." Bill and I smiled at each other for our cleverness. We had our yard back.

Lee loved to follow Bill cutting grass in the backyard. Lee marched behind him with a child's lawnmower. Its constant CLACK, CLACK, CLACK was annoying. At my request the annoying clacker disappeared as Lee mowed every day with or without Bill. I didn't know at that time that Lee's allergies should keep him from cutting grass. I felt like an irresponsible mother every time he sneezed.

We could enter the garage from the backyard where a well-stocked upright freezer sat. We bought a side of beef each winter. I was thankful I could keep our food budget low by buying in bulk. We also bought frozen fruits and vegetables in ten- and twenty-pound boxes. I'd call whomever was in the house to help bag the produce. I'd give each person a large spoon and a plastic bag to fill three-fourths full and pack them in the freezer. Sometimes those filling the bags weren't Hannas. The kids' friends were workers willing to do something unusual at the Hanna House. When I needed a bag of fruit or vegetables for a pie or a meal, I'd call a Hanna to "go to the south forty," referring to property away from the house.

Once, and only once, someone named "I didn't do it" left the freezer door ajar. Fortunately the shelves weren't completely full, but some food was spoiled. "I didn't do it" and his brothers were ordered to throw away smelly food and clean the shelves. In the spring when the power went out on our side of the street, the boys toted our frozen food in a wagon across the street to store it in the neighbor's freezer, and left a package of food as our thank-you.

One Fourth of July our family came back from the town's parade and the neighborhood kids decided to continue the parade at our house. One of the girls, wrapped in a sheet, carried a toilet paper torch with an aluminum foil flame and wore a white paper crown. She stood on a chair at the curb as the Statue of Liberty. The others sat at her feet waving. Heil Drive was a well-traveled street, and people honked car horns in passing. I enjoyed watching the girls showing their pride and taking turns dressed as the symbol of our country. I'm not sure our neighbors enjoyed the cars honking.

After watching another Fourth of July parade, we couldn't find five-year-old Jay. We looked around where we were standing and asked if anyone had seen him. Our neighbor, an auxiliary police officer, came by and asked if he could help. He knew Jay. He and Bill scoured the parade area. Frantic, I went home with Stephen, the baby at the time, to await phone calls from someone who found Jay. No one called. Jay was eventually found under one huge tree at the Memorial Cemetery where the parade ended. He wasn't afraid. He did what we told him. "If you are lost, stand by a tree."

A lamppost standing at the end of the driveway gave Hanna information to the neighborhood. As the family grew, a blue or pink balloon announced a new baby. The congratulatory phone calls would start. "I saw your lamppost. What's the baby's name?"

We received congratulations in the mail from people we didn't know. They'd sign their names as those who drove by the house every day on the way to and from work, or saw our growing family in church.

Pink or blue envelopes came and the letter carrier knew our news. Flowers came from friends and family and florists in town knew our news. Then the diaper service truck came and all who traveled Heil Drive knew our news. I felt I was living in a fish bowl.

Others noticed our house. One spring I planted gold and orange nasturtiums in front of the shrubs lining the front porch. The flowers were plentiful and accented the colors of the bricks. One day the doorbell rang. I answered it, and at my door stood an older woman wearing a loose housedress and a head scarf. I'd never seen her in the neighborhood. Frightened, I propped the door open with my foot and took a deep breath, ready to send her away and call the police.

"Your flowers are beautiful," she said. "What are they?"

I felt relieved that she seemed interested in my flowers and not my family. "Nasturtiums," I said. "Why?"

She answered, "They complement the house well." I thanked her and shut the door amazed that I, who knew nothing about landscaping, had planted something that fit the property! My fear returned when I began to wonder if she had an accomplice and was staking out the neighborhood for a burglary.

Some days I opened my door to a delivery person with a package for someone in the neighborhood. For a few years I was the only stay-at-home mother on our end of the street. Mothers went back to work when their children started school, and I was the school's contact person for their children and the receiver of their packages. We trusted each other.

Many times I thought about returning to teaching, but each time, I became pregnant. I thought God was telling me I was a better mother than a teacher.

In the 70s our children walked the quarter mile to school on our side of the street. People living along the route kept an eye on them. I was thankful my children were being watched along the way. Neighbors would call and say, "The boys are playing in the creek today," or, "Expect a call from school. They're going to be late again."

The first days of school were beautiful fall days and I walked each child to elementary school and pulled little ones in a wagon. When Stephen started first grade and was gone all day, he carried a packed lunch and milk money.

Three-year-old Kristin wanted to carry a lunch box and money too. I packed two lunch boxes with peanut butter and jelly sandwiches and apple slices that day. Kristin sat in the wagon behind baby Roy, clasping her lunch box and proudly telling him, "I'll be going to school all day someday, too!"

Two years later, I walked Kristin and her lunch box to school and pushed Roy in the stroller. Two years after that I walked Roy and his lunchbox to school and returned home alone. I felt sad every first day of school, sending our last child away from home and missing teaching and the friends I made in my teaching years, but as I walked down Heil Drive by myself, I breathed in the freedom.

Heil Drive is a throughway from Hamilton Road on the east and Route 62/Mill Street on the west. We residents formed a neighborhood that cared for each other. I felt secure when Bill traveled and I was alone with the kids. Teens from homes on the street became our babysitters.

Family was important to all of us and we could have fun. Frequently, five of us women would go out to dinner. We called ourselves the "Heil Drive

Irregulars." Neighborhood birthday parties and holiday parties were shared. When little ones wanted to play with someone on the other side of the street, they knew they couldn't cross alone. They would stand at the curb and call, "Cross me. Someone cross me."

We had found an established neighborhood to live in and raise a family. Would we fit in?

Spinning Free

Free in the fields of Grandpa's farm,
I flee the barnyard where
Yesterday I rode the old horse,
Chased chickens from trees,
Floated free as a child.

Today, my hair flying free
Like the brown ponytails I had
I spread my arms and spin in the sunlight
Waving my arms again
Like the butterfly I pretend to be.

Barn buckled, house hollow,
Fields forgotten, soon to harvest houses.
Today the land is mine
To fly, spin, sing
Grandpa's girl again.

Will new homeowners know
This grass was my spinning field?
Will they know that a little girl
Loved her summers here?
That butterflies knew her secrets?

Tomorrow, Grandpa's acres
will become Monarch Manor.
With new Grandpa's girls
To greet returning butterflies
And follow,
        Flying,
            Singing,
                Spinning free.

CHAPTER
THREE

Enter at Your Own Risk

*"Come on in," I called, opening our front door to a
neighbor and her male friend.*

*They came to pick up her daughter, Beth, who stayed
with us after school.*

*I stood in the foyer holding a baby, another child fol-
lowed me and another ran into the hallway with Beth.*

*"They're coming out of the woodwork," the man said
as he stepped back.*

"These are my children," I said. I wanted to slap him.

Entering our house, no one knew what they'd find.

The powder room was diagonally across from the front door. One night,
a visitor at our door would have seen Bill crouched on the half bath's floor in
front of the toilet, his knees to his chin, his ear to the phone, tugging at a toilet
while calling his father in Pennsylvania. "How do I get a toilet apart?" he said.
"Someone threw a diaper in, flushed it and stopped up the whole works!"

And I heard, "Mommy, Pop's playing in the potty!"

Bill wrenched the bowl off the floor, held up the dirty cloth diaper and asked his father, "What do I do now?" His dad told him to buy a beeswax ring to seal the toilet base on the floor. Bill went out and bought two rings to have an extra one on hand for the next emergency. I was amazed that someone other than a plumber could fix a toilet.

I realized in succeeding years how handy my husband was when I heard friends say how much repairmen charge for household calls, parts and labor. I place my trust in Bill when he says he can do a household repair. He repairs and improves things and the family is thankful for his abilities. (Years later when Lee was a homeowner, he asked Bill for the same advice. Lee's toilet was stopped up and he called Bill. Together they removed the culprit in his toilet; a set of upper false teeth.)

The front hallway led into the family room where the view corresponded to the ages of the children. When the kids were little, a toy box sat on one wall, then a piano when the older boys took piano lessons. Beyond there sat a rust-colored upholstered rocking chair in front of an overstuffed bookcase. I loved to read and nurse my babies in that chair. I was like Agatha Christie's character Miss Marple, who observed all and knew all. I could observe the hall activities and the front door.

At that front door, the first year we lived on Heil Drive, we saw an overwhelming number of trick-or-treaters. We were told later that they came from farms immediately east of Hamilton Road. (Housing developments hadn't been built there yet.) We ran out of candy and started handing out apples we had brought back from a visit to an orchard in Pennsylvania.

One of the trick-or-treaters asked, "Is there a razor in this?" I was shocked and angry that he would ask about my treat. This happened in the 70s when a scare from candy being injected with items sent parents to the ER to have candy x-rayed. As a mother and a teacher, I was incensed to be suspected of doing harm to children!

Another Halloween Bill and I held an adult party for the neighbors. We insulated the walls of the first floor, and furniture stood covered in the center of the rooms. Invitations said, "Come in costume." Bill and I met guests at the front door as pumpkins, wearing orange sheets with elastic at the top and bottom. The boys stuffed our costume with newspapers. We waddled around all evening.

We took photos of each couple and gave them a flashlight to roam in the dark downstairs on a scavenger hunt. We hid things around the first floor; a set of plastic false teeth on a windowsill, a huge stuffed black cat with reflective eyes in a corner, a life-size cardboard skeleton hanging in a doorway. Bill hid in the coat closet, and when someone slid open the door, he set off a camera's flash unit. Screams came from every room as couples found hidden items. I served roast beast. Others brought scary-named foods. We giggled as we heard guests' responses to our "madness."After the party and redecorating the front hall, we hung a gold-framed mirror facing the door. The frame originally held a black and white portrait of my father at about three years old with shoulder-length blond curls. He is standing wearing a sailor suit and not smiling. When our boys saw the portrait they exclaimed, "That's Granddad? Who played every sport in high school? He looks like a girl!"

I nodded and explained, "My dad was the only boy in the family and I guess that was the reason for a large formal portrait." We removed the image, added a mirror to fit, touched up the gold frame and hung a gold shelf on the wall underneath. It became the repository for everything from keys and mail, notes and incidentals and tiny seasonal decorations. Whenever an item was missing, someone would call out, "Look on the gold shelf!"

Many visitors faced themselves in that mirror as they came through our front door. Uncle Slug, our friend Bob from the bowling league, became a good friend. He came Saturday evenings with his wife to play euchre with

Bill and me. Jay, one, and Lee and Greg, seven and five, would be ready for bed and sitting on the steps waiting for him.

Bob would walk through the door with his hand behind his back. He'd pull his hand around holding a huge rock from my flower garden. The boys would scurry upstairs when he asked, "Who wants to be rocked to sleep?"

In the late 1970s and 80s, Bill and I were involved in Marriage Encounter, a weekend away for couples to learn to strengthen their marriages. We talked about our marriage as presenters. One weekend, Fr. Kevin, an Irish priest, came to present with us at a nearby retreat house. He stayed with our family before and after the weekend. I remember his comments about a loving family.

"I would rather see worn carpeting with children running up and down than perfect carpeting that no one uses." We had worn stairway carpeting in our house!

Sitting at our kitchen table, Fr. Kevin watched me sweeping the floor, smiled and said, "Mothers are the same everywhere. My mother sweeps the kitchen floor after every meal too!"

He gave us a plaque we hung on the wall at the foot of the stairs in the hallway. It states: *"Rejoice in the Lord always; and again I say rejoice" Lots of love, Fr. Kevin (Philippians 4:4)* We know this was in the late 1970s as it is inscribed only to Bill and Peg, Lee, Greg and Jay.

When we presented these weekends away, we arranged for our kids to stay with other Marriage Encounter families. Our kids learned that we weren't the only family to wash hands before meals, have household duties and say prayers before bed. When other couples were on weekends, their children stayed with us.

As a teen, Lee came in the front door one day after school furious about an unfair grade. He flung his book bag at the wall. The bag crashed through the wall and created a huge hole. He, Greg and I stood stunned by the angry action from this calm person. When I recovered, all I could say was, "Looks like you'll learn how to patch a hole tonight." That evening we all watched as he followed Bill's instructions and repaired the wall.

Because we lived on a through street, friends passed the house during the day. They dropped in for a cup of tea or coffee, knowing I needed adult company. My friend Pat stopped by one day and I invited her in for a cup of tea. We sat at the kitchen table across from each other. My back was to the doorway. Suddenly Pat's eyes grew big. She clutched her chest and leaned back in her chair. I thought she was having a heart attack.

"Oh, Peg," she said. "Look behind you."

I spun around to see three-year-old Kristin with her face completely covered in tomato-red lipstick. Only her eyes were white.

Five-year-old Stephen came up behind her. "Look, Mom—I made her an Indian!"

He led his sister into the room as he swooped his arms in the classic move of a magician. "Ta-da," he said, showing his flair for the dramatic.

Pat dropped her mug and pushed her chair away from the table as if she were afraid of getting lipstick on her.

I blinked and swallowed. "I would like my little girl back," I said to Stephen. "Do you think you could get her? Who is that Indian?"

Kristin giggled. "It's me!"

I told Stephen where the cold cream was. "Put it on tissues to wipe off the lipstick." I told Kristin, "Keep your eyes shut, little Indian, while you're changed into a girl again."

Pat, mother of two, blinked her eyes. "Oh, Peg. How could you be so calm?"

"Did you forget I am the mother of six? I can handle anything."

Little did I know...

When other friends stopped by during the day, sometimes they found me answering the door and sinking onto the nearby steps. At times I was so tired I could go no farther than the steps to talk. During naptimes I posted a sign on the door that read: "DO NOT RING DOORBELL. Child sleeping. Please knock." I felt exhausted like I was running a continuous Punch and Judy show with one child up playing while another was down sleeping, and I had to be awake for both.

Some things actually passed through the front door. At Halloween, we would take out the window on the upper half of the storm door and pass out candy through the open space. I learned to rebuff salesmen or solicitors by opening the door and screaming, "You just woke up my baby!" or saying, "I can't talk I'm on a long-distance phone call." I didn't need their products nor their interruptions in my day.

The door brought the outside world into my family and took my family out into the outside world. I saw my role as controlling what came in and out of that door.

Writing on Wood

I write on a door
Three feet from the floor
One end on file drawers
One on three legs, not four.

On its body sits a cup of tea
Papers, pencils and free
Words written by me.

But as my space
It serves a place
To write and retrace
Memories, fears and joys I face.

Some think I'm a nut.
Doors are to open and shut
In this case, it lays
Flat as it was cut.

Photos and books stand on end
In a rolling chair, hours I spend.
Words spill out on paper. I bend
To edit stories and poems I've penned.

A sliding door that's been
Protecting clothes unseen
Holds now a writer's dream
Written on paper its wood is clean
This door a portal for words.

CHAPTER
FOUR

Family Room Floor

"Leave your toys on the floor tonight. Pop's traveling."

"Anyone who breaks into the house might kill them-selves falling over the mess," I said. "We would hear them and call nine-one-one before they reach us," I assured the kids. They were happy to comply.

Toys were my alarm system.

Just in case, I kept an eight-cell flashlight beside my bed to defend my castle. I felt protected. I had a weapon to use against an intruder. I would blind and then hit him.

"You need to be quick," Bill warned me. "Someone could grab the flash-light and use it against you."

Confident I could defend my family, I would not be scared. I would be angry. How dare someone invade my home!

❖ ❖ ❖

Toys ruled the family room. Bill built a toy box in the shape of a boxcar. Painted yellow, it had a red roof, sliding doors and sat on wheels. It was big enough to hold piles of toys and hide small children. "How appropriate," people would exclaim, "that Bill would build a train car!" The roof became the starting gate of an orange racetrack for matchbox cars. Lee and Greg would attach the starting gate to the lip of the roof and send cars through a loop and out onto the track spread across the family room floor. I watched their races and wondered if we had future engineers in the family.

An indoor slide Bill made sat in the middle of the room. It had three steps up and a hinged slide in front. Kids would wear themselves out climbing up and sliding down with cries of, "Watch me." The slide became a roof to hide under and I'd hear, "Mommy can't see us here." It became a ramp for matchbox car races, "Let 'em go," and a table with the slide propped up, "I'm hungry." I loved listening to children's conversations while I worked in the kitchen, and glanced in to see them change the slide's shapes.

The family room housed a train. When I mopped the kitchen floor, I moved all the kitchen chairs into the family room and lined them up as train cars. When they were preschoolers, Lee and Greg would sit stuffed animals in kitchen chairs. Winnie the Pooh sat behind a huge Easter bunny. Raggedy Andy sat behind Oscar the Grouch. The boys sat in front wearing blue and white striped railroad caps, acting as the engineer and fireman. They would make the sounds of a steam engine, including its whistle, and call out, "We're going to Grandma's."

A decade later in the 1980s, Stephen and Kristin rode the same kitchen chair train as preschoolers with teddy bears, Pound Puppies and Cabbage Patch dolls. I would talk to them as I had their older brothers as I mopped the kitchen floor. Happy again to give them imagination time and keep them out of the way.

The train faced bookshelves flanking the fireplace. Double rows of the yellow spines of *National Geographic* magazines collected from our early married years lined the bottom shelves. They were great icebreakers for those entering our home for the first time. Upon seeing the rows of yellow many visitors exclaimed, "Oh I remember those," or, "Those were in my doctor's waiting room."

In his preschool years, Lee lined the magazines on the floor as a highway for his matchbox cars. The road ran through the family room, hallway, living room and dining room. The kitchen floor was off limits. I was always busy there. Lee would announce where his cars were according to the area on the front cover. I'd hear, "I'm in the jungle. Now I'm in a big city" or, "I'm coming home." I marveled at his imagination and am thankful my children had the experience of playing with household items as opposed to having their heads buried in today's electronic games.

As Lee and Greg grew older, they took piano lessons. A piano replaced the toy box. I wanted them to be able to read music. They took lessons for a few years, but hated to practice and to play for an audience in a spring concert.

Lee approached me and said, "I don't have to be the one to carry on Grandma Leis' musical talent." He surprised me with his understanding of the situation. I had to agree and ended his lessons.

I always enjoyed having the piano tuner come, and asked him to play his specialty, jazz, before he left. I loved to hear our piano played beyond basic finger exercises. Anyone who came to the house and knew how to play piano was not to leave until they played a number. The music reminded me of times when my mother played for me. I wanted our children to hear the piano played well.

Grandmas slept in this room when they came to visit. We bought a fold-out couch for the grandmas' bed. After the sofa bed was delivered, two-year-old Lee walked around and around the couch, lifting the cushions and looking underneath.

"What are you doing, Lee?"

"Looking for Grandma."

I spent six weeks lying on that couch. In late summer 1979, in the early stages of pregnancy with Stephen, I started hemorrhaging. At the same time The Great Gahanna Flood gushed water into our area. Heil Drive was under a foot of water. Men paddled from house to house in a canoe. Bill went out to help neighbors with their flooded sump pumps.

I was alone and in trouble. Frightened that I would lose my baby, I called a neighborhood couple. He was a doctor. She was a nurse. They came and laid me down on the "grandma couch," propped up my feet and called my obstetrician, who said to get to his office immediately. The word went out to the neighbors and one volunteered to take me in his pickup truck, which sat up high on huge wheels. I knew I couldn't climb up into that monstrous vehicle. I'd wait.

A few days later when I did see the obstetrician, I was ordered off my feet for six weeks. An internal vein had ruptured in my pelvic area from the weight of the baby. (After the first trimester, we were OK. A healthy Stephen was born in March 1980 in an uncomplicated delivery.)

Evelyn, an older lady who had raised her family, came to clean house for us while I was off my feet. She stayed on and came to clean house until she retired. A series of cleaning ladies followed over the next several years. I knew that underneath the mess, the house was clean. I realized that I couldn't keep the house neat AND clean and needed help.

For my birthday in the fall of 1979, I asked for a sliding glass door. I wanted to see the world while I was immobile. The old door had fogged up and was too cloudy to see through. Never before immobile, I had a hard time asking for help. Bill and I had no brothers and sisters to step in. Friends and neighbors became our family. They brought in food, took boys to activities and helped with housework.

I was helpless on the couch and Bill was tired after working all day. A neighbor volunteered to drive Jay to and from preschool with her little girl. Bill got the older boys off to school in the morning. After school, the boys helped by taking turns doing laundry and helping Bill clean up the kitchen after meals sent by friends. Bill and I were overwhelmed, and grateful for their caring.

In later years the family room changed. One spring Sunday we moved all the furniture, unloaded the floor to ceiling bookcases and stuffed all the family room contents into the front hall to await scheduled delivery of new carpeting. We carved a small path to the front door. Bill left the next morning for a three-day business trip. Big and pregnant with Kristin, I maneuvered through the pathway to send the boys off to school.

Two-year-old Stephen and I waited all day for the delivery. I called the salesman several times and was told the carpet was coming. Nighttime came and no carpet appeared! The next day we wound through the furniture in the hallway to get the boys off to school again. I called the salesman this time and told him, "If I don't get the carpet today, you can keep it!"

At noon, he drove up in a convertible with the rug strapped across the seats. He hefted the rolled rug over his shoulder and carried it into the house. He dropped the carpet and rolled it out in the bare room. His face was scarlet, he was panting and I feared he'd die in my house. I felt sorry for this man I had been angry with the day before. I made him sit and drink a glass of water. We apologized; me for my nastiness and he for the late delivery. I don't remember how the carpet was installed.

Folding card tables and chairs sat behind the couch in the family room ready for weekend card games with friends. Some weekdays they were covered with blankets as tents. Winters the family room card table held a jigsaw puzzle usually finished in a week. Anyone who came into the room put a piece in place. Kids learned quickly not to play underneath the table. Someone screaming, "Look what you did!" scared them away the first time they bumped the table and puzzle pieces flew.

Many Friday nights when Jay was still in elementary school, his friends brought flashlights and sleeping bags and made a tent city of card tables, couch cushions and blankets. They would eat popcorn and play cards under the tents lit by their flashlights. I was happy to host these overnighters. I knew where my son and his friends were.

❖ ❖ ❖

In the 1970s and 80s Hannas smiled at us from portraits over the fireplace in this room. At one time, a poster-size gold framed portrait of John Clark Hanna on his wedding day in the 1890s hung centered above the mantel, reminding us of past Hannas. Years later, I wondered if his stern bearded face scared the children. He was replaced in later years by a 1975 portrait of Lee, Greg, and Jay wearing blue and white striped bib overalls and railroad caps. One-year-old Jay sits in front with a large scratch on his forehead, an injury he'd acquired the day before the photograph. Ten years later one of Stephen, Kristin and Roy wearing RR clothes replaced the older boys' portrait. Stephen liked to tell all, "Look, I am wearing same overalls and shirt Lee wore."

The children faithfully hung stockings from the mantel on Christmas Eve. One Christmas present was too big for a stocking. Bill had built a kitchen set for Kristin, but before she could get to it, her teenage brothers tossed the accompanying plastic plates across the room as Frisbees. I was excited to have a little kitchen for my daughter to play in, but in a photo two-year-old Kristin's face is scrunched. She is about to cry as a plate flies past her. "Stop!" I yelled. "Now help her arrange the sink, microwave, stove and plasticware and sit while she 'cooks' in her kitchen and serves you 'food.'"

Most Christmas Eves, we went to the Children's Mass after dinner. One evening each family was to bring bells. We took the family sleigh bells. Our large brass bells rang in clear rich tones adding color to the tinkling of others' bells.

Our five heavy copper bells hang on a yoke given to a teamster who helped another. Bill's ancestors ran a freight business between Greensburg and Pittsburgh, Pennsylvania and received the bells for their help. We treasure this unusual inheritance.

Our parents took turns coming to our house for Christmas. When my parents came, I always made sure my Presbyterian mother attended Christmas service with our Protestant friends. Bill's parents went to mass with us.

One December when I was eight months pregnant with Jay, I was scheduled to read the Scripture at mass. I asked the pastor if I would be a distraction because of my condition.

He answered, "Isn't this what the season is all about?" Unknowingly, I became a model for the Christmas season.

Beyond Christmas, the family room—its happenings and changes—clearly showed the mood of the Hanna household. The family room truly became our family's room. It outgrew toys, a piano, a bed, and became a sitting room with the couch in front of the fireplace where we could sit before a roaring fire, enjoying the view outside through a clear glass door, or read a book in one of the swivel rockers.

Family-less Room

I recently read of
A family-less room
Built for a now absent family.
Did they move?
Divorce?
Become empty nesters?
What happened is hidden there.

Large screen TV hangs black upon the wall.
Battered recliner sits upright.
Couch pillows comfort no one.
Coffee table holds only white rings.
The room is dark and silent.
Why?

The kitchen is alive twice a day.
Silently one person eats there.
Dining room serves no one.
The front door stands unused.
One of four bedrooms is slept in
Adding to the family-less-ness.

Larger family no longer visits
Their activities now memories.
Sadness prevails.
One left behind ignores the family room.
No longer finds happiness there.

How long will the room be family-less?
Do rooms experience loss too?
Awaiting another family.

FIVE

Peanut Butter on the Wall

"I wonder what would happen if... "

Lee, the quiet one, and Greg, the daring one, were a good tag team.

Lee would say, "I wonder if..." and Greg would take the challenge.

One lunchtime the boys were sitting at the table. Lee said, "I wonder how far peanut butter would fly off a spoon?" Before I could intervene, Greg, sitting across from him, loaded his spoon, held it high and flung peanut butter off the spoon. The lump shot across the table and stuck to the wall behind Lee, leaving a circle of brown oil spreading on the wallpaper. My floral wallpaper was damaged. To hear them laughing at what I thought was disaster was even more maddening.

"Look at this!" I yelled. "Look at what you've done!"

The boys slid off their chairs.

"Don't move!" I said, as I prepared to stand spread-eagle in front of the mass and protect the wallpaper from further damage.

They jumped back onto their seats when I shouted, "What did you think would happen?"

The peanut butter stain remained for years. It still irks me to think about that oily stain dotting the wall.

The kitchen table became the scene of other disasters. "You know in China people give a good burp when they have been satisfied with a meal," Lee stated. At the end of the meal Greg gave a loud burp. After all their shenanigans, I should have anticipated this.

Bill was no help as he fell off his chair laughing! I scolded all three of them! Many times I wondered how I would ever instill good manners.

We started eating meals at a round kitchen table in a corner. As the family grew, a feeding table for the baby fit in the corner. With its seat sunk into a low tabletop, it took up more space than a high chair. It forced the family table to the middle of the floor. The feeding table became a permanent fixture. Baby food constantly fell and stuck to the floor underneath and the area became harder and harder to keep clean. Bill's solution: "Someday I'm going to build a drain under that table and hose down the corner after every meal."

One of the first appliance changes made in the kitchen was to sell the avocado electric stove. I learned to cook with gas and wanted to continue in my own home. We advertised the sale in the local paper. Within days a couple called to buy it. We set up a 7:00 p.m. appointment and waited and waited. They came around ten in the evening. New to the area, I had given them the wrong street names to find us. They were not happy when they arrived. I mumbled an apology and they bought the stove.

We had another reason for buying a gas stove. Late afternoon spring storms in the 1970s caused the electricity to go out many times in Gahanna. I had to think on my feet for ideas for meals. Bill is a meat and potatoes man and doesn't like cold sandwiches for suppers. My solution was to call him at work in Columbus to pick up a pizza on the way home. He found the one restaurant in Gahanna that had gas ovens and bought their pizzas. At least he had a hot meal.

I spent most of my time at the kitchen window above the sink fixing or cleaning up after a meal. I could see the children playing in the backyard. Every spring I had a sore throat and laryngitis. After a few years it dawned on me that I was opening the window above the kitchen sink to hear the kids playing outside. The air from the open window hit me at neck level. "Give your voice a rest," the doctor said. I laughed at his remedy for a mother running a household. In future springs I watched children through a closed window.

I could turn from the sink and bump into a chair at the table. Exasperated, I declared, "We need more space in this kitchen." Bill designed and built a wooden bar out from the wall with a drop leaf at the end to extend when needed. It replaced the round table. Under the bar were shelves for the mixer and other kitchen appliances. The boys stepped on the rungs of high swivel chairs and swung into their seats pretending they were at a "real" bar.

When Roy was little and misbehaved, his punishment was to sit in the middle of the kitchen on one of the high swivel chairs. He hated to be alone. Isolating him was punishment. He would scowl and kick and spin around in that chair for his whole "time out."

My chair, when not at the end of the bar, sat under the wall phone with an extra-long cord so I could walk and talk. I made my calls mornings when the children were occupied watching *Sesame Street* in another room. Afterward we would have lunch, take a walk and come home for naptime. I felt as tired as the children and needed a nap too or I couldn't keep my eyes open at the dinner table.

The little ones loved to take turns sitting under my chair at the wall phone, reaching out between the rungs and selling pieces of colored paper.

"Tickets. Come get your tickets," they called from their "ticket booth." This game kept little ones busy where we spent most of our days. Sometimes I felt isolated from the world in that room, always cooking or cleaning up with a little one or two underfoot. I escaped by reading. I read stories in Reader's Digest Condensed Books, the only ones for which I had time.

The bottom drawer of the kitchen cabinets near the refrigerator was filled with small toys and magnetic letters. The older children learned to spell with the letters, and in later years posted the day's dinner menu on the refrigerator. There is a photo of one of the boys as a toddler sitting in the kitchen drawer. Another shows a happy eleven-month-old Roy seated in a Christmas basket on the table. We had just received a basket of fruit as a present and the boys sat their brother in it. I couldn't help but laugh at their "gift basket."

Fussy time for babies was always dinnertime. It took me until the last three children to realize that I could sit the baby in a swing in the dining room doorway into the kitchen while we ate. The baby could see the family at the table, have fun swinging and sometimes fall asleep. I always thought the babies knew when I would be busiest and that's when they demanded to be fed. Before the days of the swing in the doorway, I ate with one hand and held a baby with the other. I was at my lowest weight; I didn't have time to eat a full meal!

When Bill traveled several days at a time, I was exhausted and went to bed when the kids did. I asked Bernice, the elderly neighbor across the street, to give me a 6:00 a.m. wake-up call in the morning. She was happy to have something to do as she rarely slept. There were times when I didn't hear my alarm go off at 6:00 a.m. after I'd been up with a sick child during the night, stayed awake listing the next day's schedule, or worried about a child's school issue.

Bernice would call again at 6:30 if she didn't see any lights on in our house. She knew I had to get out of bed to reach the phone. One morning I was pleased that things were going well. The boys had eaten breakfast and left for school on time. I went upstairs to get the little ones up and realized that Jay was still in bed! I felt like a terrible mother. I could have sworn I gave him breakfast and kissed him on his way out the door! I woke up Jay, gave him breakfast, strapped Stephen and Kristin in their car seats still wearing their pajamas and drove Jay to school.

They bounced up and down in their seats. "Are we going to school too?"

Sitting at the table with the children eating hot dogs and beans were times when I resented Bill's traveling. I would feel sorry for myself knowing Bill was probably eating steak with a client. When I mentioned this to him he said, "I would rather be at home." He added, "Being out of town is stressful. Meeting new clients, driving in an unknown city, staying in different hotels and eating three meals a day in a restaurant gets old." He continued, "I would rather be at my desk designing or in the lab testing ideas than selling them."

I had to remember his stress when he traveled. I could accept my hot dogs and beans or cook foods the kids and I liked. Yet, I was ready to go out to eat on weekends after being home all week. Bill was not. He was tired of eating in restaurants. We had to compromise and go out Friday or Saturday night, not both in one weekend.

It was hard "running the show" alone when Bill traveled. I didn't mind when he was gone for a few days, but times when he was gone for weekends were hardest. I needed his help. There were more demands on me. After dinner, Bill and I would usually look at each other and ask, "Kids or kitchen?"—putting kids to bed and overseeing homework or cleaning up the kitchen. With him gone, I had to do both.

In 1983 when I was pregnant with Roy, I ran the show alone for two, three-week periods while Bill was on a project in North Dakota. Having Lee and Greg in high school and Jay in elementary school was a big help with Stephen and Kristin.

The boys had "Kitchen Duties" posted on the refrigerator. They each had days to set the table and clear off the table. It was not unusual to hear, "It's not my turn. It's his turn. He traded." They also took turns reading bedtime stories to the younger ones. Bill came home at the end of three weeks, and then was back out of state for three weeks to complete the project.

I was exhausted, but I had to be strong for my family and for a newly-wed wife whose husband was on the same project. I invited her over for several meals. I wanted to show her wives could survive long stretches of time without husbands, but it wasn't easy being cheerful when I was weary.

That same year at Thanksgiving, Cabbage Patch dolls were the rage. A Columbus store announced a big shipment had arrived. After dinner one evening when Greg was learning to drive, I asked him to drive me there. We bought two dolls as Christmas presents for the youngest children; Eli for Stephen, and Trixie for Kristin. The dolls came with adoption papers with names included. Until Christmas, Greg would tell Stephen to ask Mommy who Eli was and Kristin to ask about Trixie. I was upset with him and told him to stop harassing me! Fortunately, Eli was a neighbor of my dad's and I could explain who he was. I knew no one named Trixie and had to remember what story I told about Trixie every time Kristin asked.

At times when I stood at the sink, teenage Greg would pass behind me and whisper, "I'm going to tell them about Santa this year."

I'd spin around saying, "No you're not! No one told you at this age." By that time, Greg was giggling in another room.

The little kids playing nearby would ask, "Told him what?"

The kitchen was my domain.

I felt qualified to be a chef, or at least a short-order cook in my own home. I cooked a massive amount of food. What I cooked for my family dinner would have been a small dinner party for my mother who only cooked for three. Our boys were always hungry. I would cook a dozen pork chops for one meal. There were no leftovers.

I took classes at a local college to learn how to freeze foods. I couldn't ask my mother. She knew about canning, not freezing. We bought an upright freezer and placed it in the garage. For many years our freezer sat filled with a side of beef—cut, wrapped, and labeled according to the cut of meat—as well as frozen fruits and vegetables. It was extremely economical for feeding teenage boys. My family preferred pies to birthday cakes. I always had fillings on hand from frozen fruits to make Bill's "meet" pies.

Once I made the common kitchen mistake. I tried to mix pudding in the blender. I didn't put the lid on tightly enough and chocolate pudding sprayed all over the kitchen. It splattered cabinets, ran down countertops and puddled on the floor. I told myself, "You deserve to spend the hours standing on a stool wiping down cabinets and crawling on the floor wiping chocolate off baseboards." I found pudding on kitchen items for days afterward. I was embarrassed that when we moved away, I saw chocolate splatters remaining under the plastic covering at the back of the stove.

Bill installed a microwave over the stove. The younger kids have recently told me that their entertainment when the older ones babysat was watching marshmallows grow and flatten in the microwave.

"Want to see a magic show?" The older boys would ask. They'd line up the three little ones on chairs in front of the microwave window. The boys would place giant marshmallows inside the oven, then set the timer.

"Watch," they said. "The white shapes will grow." They'd start the power, shut off the heat and watch the marshmallows swell and shrink at increasing times.

"We watched the little kids clap and cheer when finally a gooey white mass filled the space," the older boys said. "Then it started smoking."

"We thought it would explode. We didn't know what would happen to the oven, so we shut it off."

They made the little ones promise. "Don't tell Mom about our magic show and we'll do it again."

The boys cleaned up the heated goo and the little ones never told me.

I never suspected their entertainment. Hearing these stories makes me wonder what else happened when I was gone!

Across the kitchen our refrigerator did more than keep food cold, hold photos and schedules. It also acted as a place for punishment. When the older boys babysat the little ones and they misbehaved, the boys sat them on top of the fridge. Roy was terrified. Kristin climbed down. Just the threat of being put up there led them to behave. I would come home and find Roy sitting still as a statue on top of the fridge. I'd have a hard time getting him down. Balancing his weight and mine, I would stumble backward.

We did have fun in the kitchen. Holidays were always fun to cook for. The boys and I followed a pattern in a magazine to make a heart shaped cake with red icing for Valentine's Day. I loved being called for the recipe years later when my children had their own families.

For Groundhog's Day, I served groundhog. We thought it hilarious when we had to explain sausage as groundhog to others. This idea came from Bill's and my Pennsylvania roots and the state's "Punxsutawney Phil," the ground-hog who in February predicts six more weeks of winter or early spring by whether or not he sees his shadow.

On St. Patrick's Day, I tinted milk green. The kids didn't let me forget this tradition and wanted green milk on their cereal. Dinner that evening was corned beef and cabbage.

Dyeing eggs for Easter baskets became an anticipated project. After coloring a dozen, the older boys took turns creating the "ugliest egg" by dropping it in all the colors. I judged the results. Some years it was an easy choice. Bill and I hid eggs around the house for the "hunt" Easter morning. In later years, the older boys had fun playing Easter Bunny for the little ones.

For birthday parties, I baked train cakes; small loaf cakes lined up and decorated as train cars. The younger children preferred cakes, not pies.

Cutting out, decorating and baking Christmas cookies became an all-day project, with each child doing his/her thing with a mound of dough. I didn't mind sweeping up sprinkles on the floor, peeling icing off chairs or washing and storing dozens of Grandma's cookie cutters. I loved sharing my child-hood happy times with them. I watched my children having fun together without fighting.

During summer times, my best friend was my Crock-Pot. I could put all the ingredients for a meal in and set it to cook and take the kids to the swimming pool for the afternoon. I'd know that supper of meatloaf, chicken and vegetables or layered pork chops and sliced potatoes would be ready when Bill got home. My mother could not remember what the appliance was called and always referred to my "crack pot"!

I wished I could be the mother who relaxed poolside, read a book and tanned, but I had my eyes on the bigger kids in the big pool as I sat in the kiddie pool with the little ones. Once, upon entering the pool area, five-year-old Stephen ran ahead of me and jumped in the big pool. I dropped my bag of towels, ran and jumped in fully clothed to rescue him! I felt all eyes on me. As I emerged, I surprised myself for being so bold. "Mother-mode" took over. I didn't think. I acted. I felt relief not silly at my appearance—dripping with stringy wet hair, soggy street clothes and sopping wet shoes. I had saved my child!

I kept a statue of the Blessed Virgin Mary on the corner of the kitchen counter. I called on her many times as another mother. "How do I handle this?" was my common plea. Much of the time, Bill traveled and I had no one to hear my frustrations. It always helped to voice my concerns out loud. I prayed, "Give me guidance for a son who is bored in school," or, "Give me the strength to say no to an outside activity," or, "When can I read my book?"

The kitchen, "heart of the home," was where you could always find me.

On the Fridge

Telling stories of our lives
Scattered magnetic shapes
Hold photos on the fridge.

Birthdays, graduations
Family hellos and goodbyes
Remembered on photos on the fridge.

School times, mealtimes,
Christmases and prom times
Live in photos on the fridge.

Newspaper shots
Halloween monsters, frequent guests
Smile from photos on the fridge.

Report cards, rehearsal dates,
Each child's life
Clipped to photos on the fridge.

Travel times, phone numbers,
Duty lists and invitations
Fill gaps among photos on the fridge.

When the family's gone
I'll see them again
In ghost photos on the fridge.

Do people
Have a life
Without photos on the fridge?

CHAPTER
SIX

At the Table

"If the Hannas don't have Sunday pot roast dinner at the dining room table at six-thirty, their house will fall down."

—Heil Drive neighbor

Our kids would never know what the dining room was for if we didn't use it for Sunday dinners. As our children married, we asked them and their families to come for dinner one Sunday a month. For some, it was the only time we saw them other than family celebrations. We have fun together to this day. There are still two boys, now in their thirties, who can't sit next to each other. They elbow one another, grab each other's food and cause hilarity at the table. When they were younger I scolded them. I felt responsible for teaching manners all the time. Now I can laugh at their antics.

The dining room table became many things to our growing family.

Under the table was a great imaginary place for Lee, five, and Greg, three. They loved to play fireman. Wearing red plastic fireman's hats and red boots, they sat under the dining room table giggling and awaiting my wail as a siren. I announced in a deep official voice, "The fireplace is on fire!" The boys would run out from under the table with their big red firetruck; one sat on top, the other pushed. Once the imaginary fire was out, the boys crawled back under the table to await the siren's next wail. I can't believe I let them run through the house yelling, "Fire! Fire!"

My imagination inspired theirs. I loved inventing games and taking a break in my routine. I felt content to rely on my college education for teaching children and my inventiveness to keep my children busy and out of my way as I put away groceries, cooked a meal or ran the sweeper.

Years before, at my childhood dining room table with my mom and dad, we discussed my going to college. The decision for me to pursue a degree in education didn't come easily.

Dad said, "I hire women, spend the bank's time and money training them and they work for a short time, marry, get pregnant and quit." He continued, "That's what happens to women who work outside the home." Dad looked at me. "It'll probably happen to you too!" He shook his head. "Paying for four years of college will be wasted."

My mother stiffened in her chair. "How can you say that?" she fired back at him. "I graduated from college, taught music before and after our marriage and when I had a child." Dad had no rebuttal.

Dad compromised and agreed to pay for college for me, only when I promised I would graduate and teach for at least two years before I married. I graduated from college, taught two years before Bill and I married and three years after. My training for teaching helped me in understanding my own children. One of the ways they learn is by using their imagination and having fun. I was teaching my children by using a dining room table.

The dining room became a temporary nursery. In the corner of the room a portable crib or bassinet sat for the latest baby to sleep in, which saved me from climbing stairs to the nursery during the day. After I had cooked one big Sunday meal and sat down for the first time in hours, I heard crying in the crib behind me. I was angry at the baby for interrupting my meal and my only sit-down time. How could I be angry at a baby? I was the mother of six. I was supposed to handle housekeeping, meals and children. I took a deep breath, clenched my teeth, picked up the baby, and ate another meal one-handed with a baby on my shoulder. I wanted to scream, "Stop the world. I want to get off!"

Others did say what was on their mind. We always said prayers before meals and added something personal. Sometimes we'd hear, "Thank you, God, for the brownies," or, "Thanks for the snow day off of school," or, "Help me on tomorrow's test."

One weekend Bill and I were fighting. We weren't speaking to each other. He was in charge of an event at church and stayed there all morning and left me at home to get all six ready and drive us to church for mass. I felt abandoned. The event seemed more important to him than me. Frustrated and angry, I barked orders at the kids. None of us went to church in a good mood. At dinner that evening, one of the boys said, "And God it's about Mom and Pop not talking…" Bill and I were stunned that they'd noticed our coolness toward each other. After dinner the boys cleared the table and we excused ourselves and went upstairs to our room and resolved the fight.

Many times the kids and I played hide-n-seek in the dining room. A space between the china cupboard and the wall was a good place for me to hide. Kids ran past me as I flattened myself against the wall and was not seen. They always forgot my hiding place. I enjoyed stopping household routines—for the respite, and because I wanted the kids to see me having fun with them, not just concentrating on a clean house, or cooking a meal or correcting them.

Originally, the dining room had half of one wall papered with foil and gold embossed flowers. We decided to change the wall to a more subtle paper. Removing the foil above the chair rail seemed impossible. Late nights into mornings, Bill and I soaked and stripped off paper, gouged wallboard, spackled holes and sanded the surface to replace the paper with a smooth cream and soft blue patterned paper. Bill and I were pleased with the results. The long, hard work was worth it. When we shared our foil removal experience with others we heard, "We had the same problem with foil paper. Did you try…? I'll never do that again!"

Against this wall sat the narrow walnut Harvest table with drop down sides/leaves which fanned out to form a table for eight. We moved it to the middle of the room and raised the leaves on Sundays to seat our family and any guests. My older cousin from out of state came once for Sunday dinner. Helen Louise was speechless when our family of eight sat down around the table. "I can't believe this is you and your family," she said. "I remember you as an only child sitting at the Craig family table, and now you are this mother of six cooking and serving me at your table!" I impressed my cousin, a world traveler, right here in Gahanna.

The dining room table caused a frustrating and scary time. A salesman came to the house to measure the table for table pads at 11:00 one morning. It was time to walk our son to kindergarten. What was I to do? Leave this person I didn't know alone in my house and walk my child to school? Send my kindergartener to walk alone the three blocks to school?

Frustrated and alone in making this decision, I imagined all kinds of things happening if I made either choice. Would this stranger rob me of my belongings while I was gone? Would my son be safe on his way to kindergarten? I chose to walk him to school, all the time talking to myself. "Is that salesman putting my silver in a pillowcase and absconding with it? Is he taking everything he can fit in the trunk of his car?" I practically ran home. When I returned the car was there, and the man was writing up an order for pads for the table. I was grateful for a man who was one of the nice guys. I could have kissed him, but I counted the silver anyway!

We inherited six sets of china, crystal and silver from our parents and grandparents. We have two china cupboards full with sets of china for each of the children. I combine my set and Bill's grandmother's set on holidays. The "good stuff" needs to be used and I hope our children pass on the family tradition and learn the stories behind them.

Not all meals at the table were pleasant. At one Mother's Day dinner, the kids were asked to say something about me. One said, "If you can't say something nice, say nothing at all." I was crushed, heartsick to hear this from my child.

I ran from the table in tears and sobbed throughout the evening hours curled up on a picnic bench outside. I stayed outside in the dark reviewing my life as a mother. Was I really fit to be a mother? Was I teaching my children to ignore the feelings of others? I couldn't go back in and face my child.

When I finally did return, I fell into Bill's arms. He, too, was shocked at our child's words. He'd had a long talk with him and explained the damage he had done. The next day our son apologized saying, "I just heard that phrase in school and wanted to use it." I had to forgive him and remember that the words came from a child.

Our dining room table was used for meals for family and friends. I hope the kids will remember their Sunday dinners together and continue the custom in their homes.

IT'S YOUR TURN

Why do they fight about everything?
Chores are clearly spelled out
BUT
Someone insists he/she took kitchen duty
For someone else
IT'S YOUR TURN!
Why do simple chores become complicated?
It's not the chores, is it?
It's children needing to argue about something, anything.
WHY?
To learn to argue by practicing?
Is that why it continues?
I want to pick them up and
Put them where the job needs done
BUT
IT'S NOT MY TURN!

SEVEN

"Living Room" Stories

"Those bean bags have to go," I shouted, as for what seemed like the thousandth time, I picked up five white beans off the floor.

The three older boys loved to sink into bean bags and watch TV.

We had been warned. "Don't buy them. They'll split and spill beans everywhere."

The time had come. I found beans on the steps, in the washer and scattered throughout the house. Patching up seams with duct tape didn't prevent their escape.

I banished the bean bags to the curb.

The bean bags sat stacked in the corner of the front room. The TV sat at one end, the couch opposite. The boys loved to line up the bags and pounce on them to watch TV. The front room truly was a lived-in room. We spent a lot of time there. The room was not off limits as in days long ago when the front room was a parlor used only for Sunday company.

We bought the Disney channel. There were restrictions on shows the boys could watch. I never had to worry if they were watching what they shouldn't. They would tell on each other. After getting the kids to bed, Bill and I were usually too tired to keep our eyes open to watch TV shows. Some nights I was so tired I stumbled to bed and slept fully clothed on top of the covers.

We also had an interactive channel and voted on choices from a remote. The boys had a good time trying all the buttons. I worried that we would be charged for an unauthorized channel. That happened only once. The boys were warned, "If it happens again, you lose TV time." We learned later that we were one of the few families where the boys didn't "hack" the QUBE box to watch free pay-per-view or porn. It seemed that every other kid in Gahanna claimed to know the paper clip trick.

The couch became many things beyond a place to sit. I stored my silver chests and table pads under it. It became an oven when Lee was little. He slid pillows under it as cookie sheets and timed their stay. One of the pillows had raised embroidery which he called cookies. With couch cushions stacked upward the couch became a fort and the boys would hide behind them fending off the enemy. I loved to watch them playing, but found myself constantly calling, "No jumping!"

Our windows in this room were dangerous. Framed with heavy metal, they needed to be propped up to stay open. When Roy was a toddler and stood at a raised window with his hand on the sill, the window slammed shut and broke two of his fingers. His care involved the whole family! Roy didn't like the plastic splint taped around the two fingers. He slipped the splint off and hid it. I was determined to have those fingers heal well. I told the older ones, "I'll pay you a quarter to find the plastic form." They found it stuck in outdoor flower pots, stuffed in boots and slipped between chair cushions. Roy enjoyed playing "hide and seek" with the splint. I did not! I was afraid his fingers wouldn't grow straight again, but with the whole family's help, they are straight.

❖ ❖ ❖

We were still using the original couch, lamps and two chairs we bought as newlyweds thirty years before. They were reupholstered several times, but served our family well. "I broke a lamp," one teenage babysitter admitted. "We had a pillow fight." He paid for the replacement globe and didn't babysit for us again. I didn't think he was caring for the boys—he was encouraging their recklessness. I knew boys were active, but our house was taking a beating. I was constantly covering nicks in furniture with furniture polish, scrubbing boot marks from the small entryway floor and replacing broken drinking glasses.

The Christmas tree and train sat in the living room. There are photos of the children as babies in a playpen beside the tree. We learned the trick one year after we heard a thud followed by a child's screams. We had the universal experience of the tree being pulled over by a child. It scared us all! I rushed to pick up the crying child under the tree. "I've got the baby. Boys, get the ornaments," I yelled. "They're all over the room."

Bill yelled, "I've got the tree!"

The boys shouted, "I corralled six balls under this chair. I found a string of broken bulbs," and, "I see the angel under the TV."

Lionel trains ran in several loops around the base of the then anchored tree. The trains were Bill's boyhood trains from the 1940s, and two of mine inherited from my dad from the 1930s. Railroad cars were not damaged in the tree toppling and sat amid a miniature village with lighted buildings surrounding the track. A blue uniformed trackman stood with arm raised when the train passed, and a flat mirror sat under the tree as a lake reflecting tree lights. A Styrofoam tunnel painted in earthen colors sat waiting to cover train cars entering its mouth. Bill and I were reliving our childhood days with trains under our families' trees and giving our children the same experience. All was finally protected with the child in the playpen to the side of the tree.

As the three older boys developed into six-foot teens, they lay crowded into each other on the floor to watch TV. Elbows poked ribs and fights broke out. Furniture as well as bodies slammed against walls, and lamps teetered on end.

Watching TV together wasn't pleasant anymore.

We outgrew this room.

O Christmas Tree, O Christmas Tree

Growing or boxed through November
You stand in our homes in December.

Dressed for the holiday
You create a grand display.

Lights brighten your branches
Cause us second glances.

We remember you throughout the year
Hoping to recreate how you appear.

Live green brought in from winter's snow
Or greens unboxed, remind us of spring's show.

In winter's solstice, Christmas time of year
We bring in light, wish all good cheer.

Toast the tradition your greens bring
Honor the gift of rebirth come spring.

CHAPTER

EIGHT

Up and Down the Steps

"Sit still."

"Tell him to smile."

"Quit pinching me."

All of these phrases were heard over the years as family members sitting on the steps became a Christmas morning photograph. It started with eight-month-old Lee who was afraid to sit on Santa's lap for a photo, so I photographed him sitting on our steps to wait for Santa. Every year since, the children sit on the steps and wait to see what Santa has brought while Bill takes a picture. We're able to see the family's growth from the older boys as babies on my lap, to older boys with a brother or sister on their laps, to present day sitting with their own children on their laps. The tradition continues to this day with the same comments.

At the top of the steps a Crucifix hangs on the wall. We are a Catholic family and need to be reminded of His life and death and resurrection. The gold figure on a foot-long wooden cross was a wedding gift. The top with the Corpus slides off the cross. Underneath is a vial of holy water and a small candle to aid a priest in conferring Last Rites or Healing of the Sick. I take comfort in this constant visual of our faith.

We attended noon mass each Sunday because it took all morning to get everybody dressed and out the door! My parents taught me that how you dressed expressed how you felt about where you were, SO I insisted that all wear dress clothes to church. I felt like a drill sergeant barking orders to get everyone ready. Many Sundays we were late to church because someone called, "I can't find two good shoes!" or, "I want to stay home today," or, as getting in the car, someone would yell, "It smells in here. The baby pooped."

Members of St. Matthew the Apostle Church knew our family. We sat in a front pew so kids could see the altar. We sat near an exit door and told the kids, "If you misbehave the whole congregation will see us taking you out that door and know why!" It was not unusual to see a fussy baby being passed from Bill to me or to an older boy to hold. One Sunday as we were standing, the baby at the time was crawling around behind me in the pew and bumping into me. Upset, I reached around and swatted the child directly behind me. After mass, a friend standing behind us leaned over and said, "You swatted the wrong kid."

To the right of the Crucifix at the top of our steps was the boys' bathroom, so called before our daughter arrived. With its blue and white figured wallpaper and blue towels, the room was the scene of many screams, laughter, blood, and tears. When Lee dropped a thin, lit flashlight down the toilet, I asked him why. He answered, "To see how long it would stay lit."

Another time, he cut his forehead falling on the corner of the counter around the sink. I followed the directions on the box of bandages and applied a butterfly bandage. With shaking hands I cleaned away the blood, pinched the skin together and applied the bandage praying the whole time, "Lord, guide me to do this right so my son won't have a scar because of me."

Our children vomited in the toilet after ingesting poison and the antidote ipecac. I read a magazine article about stocking a medicine cabinet for families with children. I was the mother in the neighborhood who had the bottle of medicine to induce vomiting after instruction from Poison Control. Many children in the neighborhood vomited in their own toilets from doses of that one borrowed bottle.

All our children were potty trained in this bathroom. A small green potty chair sat under a set of shelves. Beside the potty was a stack of books. The children were to sit there until finished. Lee would read his own version of "Little Riding Red" aloud. One evening, I became my mother in that bathroom—acting like someone I thought I'd never be. Greg was in the tub splashing the walls, the floor and me. I had asked him to stop and finally yelled, "How many times do I have to tell you to stop?" like I'd heard my mother ask me.

Greg answered, "Three!" I walked out of the room before I could do bodily harm to my son. He was only answering my question!

Brushing teeth followed a song of, "Upstairs, downstairs and all around the house." The toothbrush had to go around all those places in one's mouth. Each had his/her own color-coded toothbrush and cup. The mirror above the sink saw many faces—from smiles for accomplishments, to scrunches from bad haircuts and tears after children's hurts and my tears from exhaustion. "Can I pick up one more toy, oversee one more page of homework or fold one more basket of clothes?" I'd ask the face in the mirror, and a voice from inside me said, "Of course you can. You're a mother."

Lee, Greg and Jay were bathed as infants in a small plastic tub that fit in the bath tub. When Stephen, Kristin and Roy were babies, they were bathed in a sponge shape that fit in the plastic tub. Rubber duck, boats, cups and water wheels in a plastic woven potato sack hung on the shower head. I believe they were all dumped into the water every night, so putting them away delayed bedtimes.

As a toddler, Roy slipped in the tub and fell against the spout, splitting open his chin. I carried my bleeding and sobbing child downstairs, grabbed an ice pack from the freezer and held it on his chin while Bill drove us to the emergency room. Roy was strapped to a papoose board to hold him still while the doctors stitched his chin. A few days later, I took him to our family doctor to have the four stitches removed. We came home and within minutes, Roy tripped and fell, reopening the wound. Bill had just pulled in the driveway after work. I ran outside carrying the bloody toddler shouting, "Don't turn off the motor. We have to go to the emergency room again." Once there, I hoped I wouldn't be accused of child abuse.

After exhausting days, many nights I sat on the toilet seat with three-year-old Greg on my lap. He had croup. Hot water running from the shower filled the room with steam to help him breathe. I sang songs to soothe him as he leaned against me, spent with his hooting/honking cough. Other nights, Greg and I sat propped up on his bed with a vaporizer on the floor and an umbrella over us forming a croup tent. Wisps of my damp hair stuck to my face. I didn't dare raise my hand to remove them and disturb Greg who was finally asleep. I wondered how many mothers were doing the same.

Many times I watched Lee struggle to breathe from attacks of asthma. Some of his attacks were so severe that I could fit my fist in between his ribs as he gasped. I would drop what I was doing when I heard him gasping, call a neighbor to babysit the other children or strap Greg and Jay in the car and take them with us as we rushed Lee to the doctor's for a shot of Epinephrine. Fortunately, the allergist's office was on the east side of town, exactly eleven minutes from our house.

Although Lee outgrew these attacks, he and the allergist became good friends during his weekly visits for shots. Some of his asthma attacks were allergy related. When he was tested, his allergies were the same as Bill's. I loved to say, "Lee is definitely his father's son."

When we were in Florida visiting my parents, Lee had an attack on a family outing. My mother-mode took over and I left Bill and Greg standing on the putt-putt course, while I picked up Lee and rushed him to the nearest hospital. When we returned, Bill was angry. "You didn't even speak to me," he said. "You just took Lee and left."

My response was, "You're never around when these attacks happen. I'm used to dealing with them quickly and by myself." He had to admit this was true. Many childhood crises happened during the day when he was at work or out of town.

During winters both boys had upper respiratory infections. I threatened to buy stock in the pharmaceutical company that sold the antihistamine pre-scribed. I bought dozens of bottles of the syrup; I felt entitled to royalties. I knew by then to tell the doctor what antibiotic to prescribe. One antibiotic never worked, but I had to lug the boys in for a visit before our doctor pre-scribed any medication. I hated sitting in the waiting room for hours with other coughing and sneezing kids. At one appointment I left, telling the re-ceptionist, "I'll call for another time." She called back and gave me the first appointment the next day. I needed to protect my kids from others' illnesses and learned to ask for morning appointments.

A wooden pressure gate helped with protection at home. It expanded to fit the opening leading down fourteen steps. I felt safe with it there. For many years, a child learning to walk or crawl peered through the gate. The gate in position was a necessity. Many times one of the older boys pushed on it too hard and it flew down the steps. A boy screamed. A baby cried. The wood smacked against the wall at the bottom. Bill or I rushed to the scene calling, "Anybody hurt?"

One evening, Greg placed his drawing of a skeleton for middle school sci-ence homework at the top of the steps. It was to be taken downstairs and put in his backpack. The white outline of bones was too appealing to Jay, eight.

"M-o-o-o-m, look what he did!" Greg shouted, waving the drawing in front of me.

"I made it look better," Jay said. "I put clothes on it."

"It wasn't yours," Greg shouted. "It's ruined." I felt sorry for both boys and instructed Jay to help Greg remake the skeleton.

The steps became a surprise slide when Greg left his nylon jacket hanging on the end of the banister and it slipped off. Coming around the corner, Lee didn't see the jacket on the floor, stepped on it and slid all the way down the steps on the jacket. Hearing his thuds, I ran again to the foot of the stairs to see my teenage son sitting on the floor, stunned at his quick descent. "What happened?" I helped him up. "Are you OK?"

He flexed his arms and legs. "I think so," he said. "I didn't know I could fly!"

By this time, I didn't get hysterical at my children's accidents or illnesses. Our family doctor and I had a routine. He would walk into the examining room and hold out his hand. I would slap a sheet of paper on it with questions for the child to be treated. I took it as a compliment when he commented, "You're one of the calmest mothers I see, so your children are easy to diagnose and treat."

The narrow upstairs hallway became a place for bedtime story hour. I would sit at the top of the steps and read the Narnia series to Lee, Greg and Jay. We loved *The Lion, the Witch and the Wardrobe* and the succeeding stories. In later years, as I became busier at bedtimes getting Stephen, Kristin and Roy ready for bed, I was pleased to know the older boys read the remaining books on their own. Books are important to me and I have always read to the children; at bedtimes and their quiet times. Any time the children needed quieted, I stopped what I was doing and read a story to calm all of us.

Reading aloud has been a great tool when babysitting the children of others. Friends and I organized a babysitting club. We swapped cards as payment. We printed colored cards indicating the amount of time. Red was an hour, blue was half an hour. We all started with the same amount of time cards and paid each other in cards for babysitting. I was either swamped with cards because I was home to watch the children of others, or out of cards because I had so many children to be watched. As a former teacher, I didn't mind many children in the house. They played with our toys, and learned to play with other children. Mommies could get away for doctor's appointments, shop or have lunch with friends. Most of the children were toddlers and went to school or preschool in the following years and the group disbanded. I felt safe leaving my children with other mothers and was glad to know others felt safe leaving their children with me.

We hired babysitters for long stays away. Older women in town were referred by friends who had hired them to watch their children. Once a year I went on a trip with Bill. Engineers' conferences were held in different cities around the nation and he attended or presented a paper at these sessions. I went with him for a long weekend when in the States, or for a week when abroad in Germany, Switzerland and England. I told everyone, "This annual trip becomes my shot in the arm for a year. I look forward to acting like a lady, not a mommy."

On these trips, I went with wives on city tours or shopping trips during the day. I met other couples with Bill for dinner in the evenings and shared in adult conversations. I met and discovered many interesting people and places; viewed the Arch in St. Louis, toured Nashville and the Grand Ole Opry, walked Atlanta's Underground, ate in San Francisco's Chinatown, and shopped in New York City and Chicago's Miracle Mile. I would see none of these places on my own and was excited that Bill loved me enough to take me on these trips.

Once we missed a connecting flight in France. I had to rely on speaking French to get us on another flight to Geneva, Switzerland. I surprised myself. The ability to speak French returned and we arrived in Geneva on time for Bill's meetings. At the end of that stay, we traveled by train from Switzerland to Germany through the Black Forest. Unfortunately, it rained the whole trip and we didn't see the forest's beauty. We were not expecting to see a part of Americana when we emerged from the train. Facing the station was a McDonald's!

Photos of the boys show them sitting at home on the steps waiting for us when we came home from our grown-up trips. They had their stories, too. "Guess what she did. She cooks different stuff. We missed you."

The stairs also became a scene of punishment. Jay sat there for what we now call "time out." He couldn't stand to hear others playing and not see them.

As a teenage driver, Greg missed a curfew and didn't call home. He arrived home to face an angry Bill and the loss of driving privileges. Greg pleaded for the car for another night. He was a member of the stage crew for an ongoing play. Bill held out my large flashlight, pointed to the hall steps and stated, "You will have all four cheeks—face cheeks and butt cheeks—on these steps at eleven o'clock tomorrow night." He waved the flashlight. "Or else."

The next night Greg made sure Bill knew when he arrived home. He stomped into the house, slammed the door and sat on the steps one minute before eleven. "See?" he said. "All four cheeks."

Our rule for driving the car: "If not home by eleven o'clock, call at eleven and let us know where you are. If you call, you may get another half hour, if you ask. If you do not call, you lose driving privileges for the next time you want the car." We awaited the 11:00 check-in calls when the boys were out at night, and applied the rule to younger kids when it was their turn to drive. Only one abused the rule and lost privileges.

Wallpapering the wall beside the steps almost ruined our marriage. We had decided on striped paper to match the color scheme of the living room. Bill stood on one step pasting the paper and I stood on another step trying to hold up the paper to match the stripes. It became a nightmare! Paper curled and ripped as we bumped into each other. "I can't reach as high as you."

"Just stand still where you are," he'd say. "Quit moving around." The children heard us trying to help each other and ran up and down the steps watching us.

After much snapping at each other, Bill and I decided that I should leave with the children. We spent a fun day wading and skipping stones in the creek at a nearby park. Bill finished the job in peace. I felt redeemed for my clumsiness. I helped by being away from the job and keeping the kids from learning any more foul language.

Who knew a set of steps could be so integral to a family's life?

Christmas Cards/Paper Friends

Reliving the past through
Year-old Christmas cards,
I compose this year's list
From paper friends.

Poinsettias, trains, carolers,
Manger, snowmen, and pines
Printed "Season's Greetings"
With personal messages added.

Annual news and photos,
Highlights of months behind
Reminders of life
With old friends.

Scanning aging faces,
Children now adults,
Reports of families expanding
Familiar voices speak.

Empty nesters, blended families
Grandparents, grandbabies,
Weddings, births, deaths,
Similar lives shared.

Annual connection to far away friends
Recalls former times.
Their frozen faces await
Christmas letters and photos
I send.

NINE

Whose Bedroom?

"Mo-o-m!" Many times I heard this plea as boys shared a bedroom. "He destroyed the model I built."

"He tore a page out of my book."

"My markers are missing again."

These daily reports frustrated all of us.

As the family grew, the occupants of the four original bedrooms changed at a dizzying pace. We shuffled and reshuffled the two small and two large rooms and eventually added an additional bedroom over the garage.

When we moved to Heil Drive, Bill and I slept in the master bedroom with the attached bath at the back of the house. It was our private space and served us well for thirteen years. The door had a lock that required a key. When Jay asked where the key was, we didn't know. The door had never been locked until Jay pushed its button. Angry to be locked out of my own room in my own house, I shouted, "WHY did you do this?"

Jay sheepishly said, "I thought it would help find the key."

Bill called a friend and the two of them unlocked the door. We did find the key. Later we used it to keep kids out when we wanted privacy.

The long front bedroom became Lee's where he slept in his first big boy bed. He turned two the April we moved in. I took him for his checkup and measles shot. He was the one in a million who caught the measles from the shot!

I was five months pregnant with Greg and scared to death! I had heard stories of measles affecting the development of organs in a fetus. Would my child be blind or deaf? Disabled from my exposure? I had both types of measles; once as a child and again as an adult. Was I immune?

When I finally swallowed my fears and called the obstetrician, he said, "You've passed the first three months and there should be no harm done to the developing baby." I said a silent prayer of thanksgiving and breathed a sigh of relief. Later I realized the doctor was also reassuring me so I could continue the pregnancy without worry. Greg was born a healthy eight and a half pounds the following August.

The smaller back bedroom became the nursery. It seemed that the crib, chest of drawers, changing table and rocker never left that room. One child, who will remain unnamed, took off a dirty diaper, jumped up and down in the crib and flung poop all over the room. I was furious and close to tears seeing the messy child and the brown dotted room, knowing that I had to clean it. For days I scrubbed poop out of the white woven wicker changing table, and hosed it down in the backyard while muttering, "The one who pitched this mess should be cleaning this up, not me."

When Greg was a toddler, he still slept in the nursery. He never took naps, and spent afternoon "quiet time" playing in his room when he should have been taking a nap. Lee was a good sleeper and I expected Greg to be also. He was not!

When I asked the doctor about Greg not sleeping as well as Lee, he asked, "What makes you think he needs as much sleep?" I didn't have an answer. Thus, Greg's afternoons became "quiet times not nap times." We put a wooden folding gate across the doorway to keep him in his room. He didn't want to be there and wasn't sleepy, but I needed the nap! Greg pushed over the gate only once! The wooden gate crashing on the wooden floor scared us both!

Greg would sit at the gate and call for help from anyone he could think of. I thought if anyone heard my son, they might call the police.

"Grandma, help me!" Grandmas lived in Pennsylvania. "Daddy, help me!" Bill was at work twelve miles away. "Mailman, help me!" He had come and gone by naptime.

When we brought infant Jay home from the hospital in 1975, Lee, six, and Greg, four, had chicken pox. Lee had a mild case, but Greg, sleeping in the same room, caught the disease from him and both boys were covered with sores and scabs.

Chicken pox is highly contagious and can be fatal to an infant. The doctor ordered baby and me into isolation at home. I had a severe case of chicken pox when I was a teen, so I felt safe. Baby was in danger.

Jay and I were restricted to the master bedroom. My mother-in-law came to help Bill run the household. They wore masks. I felt helpless confined to the room and a little jealous that my household was running well without me. The older boys didn't see Mommy and new baby for a while. Did they miss me? Were they jealous of baby's time with Mommy? Jay and I had time to get acquainted before fitting into the household routine.

It was Jay's turn to sleep in the nursery in the family crib. Late nights I sat in the rocker and nursed him while I read a book to stay awake. I am a sound sleeper. I never heard the babies' cries from our bedroom. Bill would hear them, wake me, bring me the baby and go back to sleep. I would trudge to the nursery and feed the baby. I felt thankful that I was healthy enough to nurse my babies and watch them grow from my nourishment.

When Stephen was born in 1980, he slept in the nursery and the other front room became five-year-old Jay's. Bill built a beautiful wooden bunk bed with room underneath for a desk. Behind it the wallpaper had white spaceships soaring through dark blue skies. When Jay grew too tall to sit at his desk under the top bunk, he spread out on the floor underneath his bunk and read books. The desk sat under the window.

His room had the stairway to the attic in his closet. Jay played with Halloween costumes hung there. He loved dressing as a clown or fireman or astronaut for the day! Friends gave us complete costumes their children outgrew. We always had someone the right size for one of the costumes. The closet steps were also a good hiding place for games of hide and seek, and for someone in trouble who didn't want to be found.

When Lee and Greg were in school, we placed a hook lock high on the outside of their bedroom door to keep the little ones from getting in when the boys were gone. On my order the lock was "to keep people out, not to lock people in!"

One evening I passed the open door to the older boys' room and saw movement in the air. I passed again and saw something flying. I passed again and saw a baby in mid-air! I ran into the room with my hand over my heart thinking I'd find the baby on the floor. The boys' beds came out from opposite walls and they stood at the ends and tossed the baby across to one another.

Terrified, I screamed, "My baby! What are you doing to my baby?"

I grabbed the giggling baby, cuddled him and sat on the floor gasping for air, waiting for my heart to resume a normal beat. I began my tirade. "Don't you ever do this again!" I shouted. "This is a BABY not a plaything. Do you know what could happen if you dropped him?" and I continued ranting. By then both baby and I were crying.

The boys stood stunned by our tears and said, "Don't worry, Mom. He likes it. We've done this with every baby."

Kristin was born in late spring 1982. The previous fall, Bill and I attended training for Engaged Encounter weekends. We had presented Pre-Cana (marriage preparation sessions) and wanted to offer weekends away for engaged couples in guided reflections on their relationships.

We presented our first weekend in Columbus in early April 1982 with two other couples. We were in downtown Columbus in a building converted from a school into a dormitory for Sacred Heart Parish. I was nine months pregnant and trying to get comfortable to sleep Saturday night when we heard sirens and warnings for a tornado.

This was extremely unusual. We tried to keep our cool and herded twenty couples into the basement of the old dorm. One man asked, "Is this part of the program?"

"Are you OK?" everyone asked me as we sat on the crowded steps. "Are you going to go into labor now?"

"I'm OK," I answered, concerned more for the lives for which we were responsible than my own. I knew I always delivered my babies late.

We survived the weekend. Kristin was born at the end of the month.

After Stephen, two, tried to crawl over the nursery room visitor's window in the hospital to see his new sister, I asked to stay another day in the hospital. I knew what I was facing at home. As the boys would say, PAN-DI-MON-IUM! Having a girl in the family was a big adjustment. I had to get used to saying "she" when people asked how the baby was doing.

She slept in the nursery, which turned into a little girl's room with feminine wallpaper on one wall. Bill painted the other three pink. His comment: "Do you realize it takes three coats of girl's pink to cover the darker boy's blue?" I was excited to decorate a little girl's room! I bought a white cupboard with rods for hanging her frilly dresses. I added white tie-back curtains with ruffles, and sat a small table and chairs under the window for tea parties with her stuffed animals and dolls. I looked forward to introducing my family to a girl's world.

My childhood friend from Pennsylvania came and brought three years-worth of her little girl's outgrown clothes for Kristin. I was extremely grateful and loved dressing my daughter in feminine clothes.

My mother and my aunt made a pink and white quilt and matching pillow sham for a big girl bed. Kristin's experience of sleeping there for the first night was the same as the boys'. We put pillows on the floor at the side of the bed in case she fell out, but she rolled out the bottom!

In following years, different combinations of younger siblings shared rooms. The two older boys did well together. They stayed in the big front bedroom. We tried putting good sleepers together, but age differences caused problems. Jay cried, "Stephen broke another model I spent hours making."

Stephen replied, "I was flying it." Bill and I sympathized with both and knew we had to make another change.

The former master bedroom became Kristin and Stephen's room. Bill built a bunk bed with boards painted primary colors. In a photo, Bill is sitting on the floor in front of it reading a story. Kristin, two, sits beside him and Stephen, four, is on the bed peering over his shoulder. A life-size black stuffed panther sits on the floor beside them; a gift a neighbor girl won at the fair. This was a good arrangement until we changed again.

We decided to add a master suite when I was pregnant with Roy. It was exciting to see construction over our garage. Bill worked with the contractor in designing the bedroom, bath, office and deck. I'd never seen rooms built from scratch and watched the rooms appear as planned. When finished, bedrooms changed again.

Roy was born in 1984. He slept for a few months in the den of the addition. He graduated to the family crib in the nursery. At two, he had two broken fingers from a falling window. The first night home after the hospital visit to have his fingers x-rayed and splinted, we were instructed to "keep his hand upright to reduce swelling."

"How will we do that?" I asked the nurse who had to stand behind me with Roy screaming and kicking on my lap.

She pushed us up to the x-ray plate and told me, "Tie his hand to the slats on the side of the crib." That night I held his arm tied up to the crib side while I sat on the floor and sang him to sleep. In the morning, the wrappings, the splints and I were spread out on the floor!

At the completion of the addition, Bill and I moved into the new master suite. The oldest boys, now tall teens, moved into our previous master with its bathroom. They could get up, shower, dress and leave for high school in the mornings without disturbing the younger ones.

Bill built a double desk that fit in the room. Lee sat on one side with writing space and a set of drawers facing him. Greg sat on the opposite side with a reverse design. This monster piece of furniture sat under a window where the boys "slaved over" their homework.

In those years, extra-long beds and bedding were not easily available. I was grateful for a friend who shopped at Penney's outlet every Friday. She called me when she found extra-long sheets or blankets. "Buy them, I'll pay you back," I'd reply. "I can't meet you. I don't have the time nor the energy to pack up my active little ones."

Bill wired an intercom system throughout the house. Each bedroom had a monitor from which calls could be made and/or received. I would call from the main monitor in the kitchen, "Lee, you have a phone call," or, "Dinner's ready," or, "Someone come help me."

This system eliminated my standing at the bottom of the stairs screaming and/or waking up a baby. Our rule was, "If you wake up a baby, you put him/her back to sleep." I loved the intercom system despite the holes drilled into the walls for the wiring.

In a final effort to accommodate everyone with his/her own space, we divided the long front bedroom into two bedrooms. Stephen, seven, and Roy, two, shared the space. Roy's side had train wallpaper, Stephen's side the remaining paper from the big boys' room of USA patriotic images—the Statue of Liberty, Liberty Bell and others.

Bill built tall bookcases which divided the room, creating a bedroom with a window for each boy. The shelves opened facing Roy's side for his toys, and on the back side facing Stephen's side for his books. A folding door in the middle opened into Stephen's side. On paper it seemed a good arrangement, but Roy constantly climbed over the bookcases into Stephen's side allowing him full range of the room. "M-o-o-m," I heard Stephen yell many times as Roy broke another one of Stephen's belongings.

These daily reports frustrated all of us and became another sign that we needed more space.

I Can't See the Rug

Under my bed are wonderful things
Yellow yarn, pieces of string,
One mini flashlight, a card with a king,
Fuzzy pink slippers, one high-top shoe,
A balled up smelly white sock or two.

One purple pen, homework from school
A valentine, yo-yos; one green, one blue
A white bottle without its glue
One paper clip, and old dead bug. Ugh.
"What a mess," says Mom. "I can't see the rug."

There's Mom's lost earring, a stuffed scratchy cat,
A wadded tissue, red toothpaste cap,
My old blanket, an open city map,
One short pencil, snap together plane,
Christmas candies in a see-through cane.

"Hurry," Mom growls. "Clean up this mess.
Grandma's sleeping here. She'll be your guest."
Mom leaves. I stay here, I guess.
I flex my magic fingers and ZAP
The shoe jumps. Its laces flap.

I wiggle my fingers. Their force unites.
High-top shoe flutters around the lights.
My sister's pink slippers soar like kites.
My tricky digits bewitch the socks.
They float into the dirty clothes box.

Yellow yarn, loose string, paper clip, too
Fly into the empty bottle, no glue.
Yo-yos roll crushing wadded tissue.
Pen, pencil, flashlight zoom into their drawers.
Cat chews bug and valentine then roars.

Mom's earring spins into her room and SNAP
My finger gun blasts the toothpaste cap.
Back to the car I send the city map.
King card wraps old blanket around me.
I say, "Plane deliver candies and flee."

Plane and candy collide in mid-air.
Red and green circles fly everywhere.
I hear Mom calling, "Are you done in there?
Time to come in and check?" she asks.
Scurrying, I finish my tasks.

Everything is finally put away.
Standing and saluting Mom I say,
"I can clean a rug any old day.
Now for my magic carpet ride."
On my old blanket cape, I sail outside.

TEN

Above the Garage

"I want to see what the addition looks like from inside," I said, staring at the framework.

I was passed through an open window.

I was pregnant and couldn't crawl through the space, so Bill and friends passed me through on my back. I looked like a whale.

These rooms became our master suite built over and beyond the existing garage. The new structure was designed to raise and use the present roof trusses. Three rooms were to conform to the size of the double garage. Bill suggested cantilevering a deck beyond the addition to extend over the patio. The contractor had never done this type of construction, and he and Bill conferred and came up with a design that worked. The deck, the width of the addition, provided a private place off our bedroom where I loved to sit mornings and drink coffee. Its outside corner gave me a place to relax or monitor the kids playing in the yard below. It hid me from the world.

The builders were able to match the color of the stucco of the house. Bill fought for an extension of the roof over the outside wall, which added to the natural look of the addition. Several people driving by stopped and asked, "Who built your addition and matched the stucco so well?" We were happy to provide the builder's name. We knew we were pricing ourselves out of the neighborhood, but we needed the space.

The entry to our three rooms started at the end of the upstairs hall through the former linen closet. That entrance led to scary times. When Greg, a teen, stopped wearing a retainer to balance his teeth, he celebrated by hanging the metal shape from our bedroom doorframe. We didn't see it until we were going to bed that night. The metal contraption hit my head as I passed under it. I screamed and batted it away. "A spider in our bedroom? What's happening? Get it out of here!"

We could hear the boys giggling in their bedroom, assured that the mouthpiece had done its job. I planned to get back at Greg and hatched a plan to place the mouth gear under his pillow at a later time.

The door worked for us, too! Friends told us that Vaseline was not just for advertised use, but smeared on a doorknob, it kept fingers from getting a firm grip and could give us privacy. The teenage boys became wise to its use and knew to stay away, sometimes singing, "We know what you're doing." Saturday morning cartoons were not just for kids.

Our new bedroom was spacious enough to hold our king-size waterbed, nightstands, and dressers. Waterbeds were in style, comfortable but not fit for pregnant women to exit. I had a terrible time getting out of bed in later stages. I learned to crawl up on all fours and step out, glad I couldn't see myself in the mirror. We later drained the bed and bought a regular king-size bed.

In addition to a huge bedroom, we had a walk-in closet, bathroom and office. Floor to ceiling windows with a sliding glass door ran along the south wall. One window on the east side connected to form a corner set. A tall fichus tree sat between the two windows.

"That tree doesn't like me," Bill said. He was right. When he passed it to get into bed, he sneezed. We realized that he was allergic to the mold forming in its dirt. We sent the tree to friends who had a greenhouse. I hated to see the greenery go as it fit beautifully at the corner windows.

The bathtub and shower were installed as one piece. The structure was delivered to our backyard. "How will it get up to the second floor?" I asked, walking around walls taller than me. "You'll never get it up there." I underestimated my husband's abilities again. The one-piece enclosure was hauled up from the backyard on a makeshift ramp. Bill and three engineer friends made a rope sling and pulled it up the ramp through the gap in the framed structure where the sliding glass door was to be installed. I stood wide-eyed at this whole operation.

After the bathroom's wallboard was up, we hung mirrors at our separate heights. "I can't see all of my face in a mirror at your height." I'd always complained about mirrors and pictures placed at Bill's eye level, which was higher than mine. A no longer needed marble windowsill sat under my lower mirror. I felt pampered to have my own makeup area. A free-standing cabinet with shelves and doors underneath held our linens from the eliminated linen closet. It gave the room a sophisticated look.

The construction company put up the structure's shell. Jay was little then and donned a yellow hard hat to watch the "workermen." They enjoyed seeing Jay as he sat in the driveway and stayed out of their way.

Bill and I and boys finished the rooms, installing wallboard, electricity and plumbing. Growing up, Bill had experience working with his dad redoing a room every year in their old house. He wanted the boys to have the same experience. They helped with the plumbing; Bill sent each boy to sit at a joint with a bucket. Bill's instructions were: "I'm going to turn on the water. If you get wet, yell." No one yelled so joints were sealed.

Bill and I spackled wallboard late at night and into early morning hours.

Baby Stephen sat in a swing watching. Friends stopped by one morning around 1:00 a.m. They saw the light in the addition and came to check on progress. A photograph reminds us of our hard work that night. We were covered with spots of white spackling and looked like a popcorn machine exploded near us.

Bill and a friend, Jim, put up the ceiling and stippled the plaster. I went with his wife, Connie, to buy an all-weather coat for our upcoming trip to England. The next week, the night before the trip, Bill and I slept on the new carpet that had just been laid in the room. Our furniture would be moved in when we returned. It was relaxing to sleep on the soft floor and actually be in the finished area we had created. We were excited about our upcoming trip, and also about living in this new space we designed.

One night when Bill was gone on a business trip, I heard THUMP, THUMP, THUMP down the hallway. Terrified, I slipped out of bed and grabbed my weapon. Wielding my long flashlight I followed the thumps to the boys' bedroom where the sound got louder. When I cautiously opened the door and swept the room with the light from the flashlight, I saw Lee sitting cross-legged at the head of his bed tossing paperbacks into a box at the foot of his bed. "I can't sleep," he said.

Breathing deeply to calm my nerves, I wanted to throttle him, but I tucked the weapon under my arm, grabbed his hands and said, "From now on, please READ one of the books until you fall asleep. You really scared me."

He apologized and agreed to read until he fell asleep. When I went back to bed I couldn't sleep imagining what could have happened. I could have swung the flashlight and seriously hurt my son!

The new third room, the office/den in the addition, held bookcases along one wall and our desks opposite; a true office until it was needed for a crib. The room became a nursery for Roy and Kristin in their first months. For

Bill's birthday present one year, I ordered railroad printed wallpaper for the office. Friends came and helped me put up the surprise. Bill appreciated the effort and the paper. He could look at brown outlines of engines and RR memorabilia on cream paper while sitting at his desk. We ordered brown insulated shades for the windows to darken the room for sleeping babies.

Most times the room looked like an office except for the crib of the newest Hanna! We were glad to have the space near us for late night and early morning feedings. I could hear the early morning joggers talking as they passed our house. They never knew I was up too!

Late one spring morning I was preparing to nurse Roy in the same room. Holding him in my arms and lowering us into the rocking chair, I glanced out the upstairs window. I noticed traffic backed up on Hamilton Road, a major north-south route through Gahanna. Two children in red coats and blond hair stood in the middle of the road. I knew those coats. Stephen, five, and Kristin, three, were stopping traffic. They escaped from the house when I thought they were downstairs watching *Sesame Street*! Panicked, I threw my baby in his crib, stumbled down the steps and ran out of the house to rescue my children. Terrified, I ran through two neighbors' yards. Their fences blocked my access to Hamilton Road. Screaming, "I'm coming. I'm coming," I ran through the third yard and finally reached the side of the road where a police officer had corralled Kristin and Stephen and stood talking quietly with them. Gasping for air, I hugged my children, and dropped to the ground. I stuttered, "I'm Mom." I looked up at their rescuer. "Thank you," I said.

Between gulps of air and a wildly beating heart, I asked my two runaways, "What were you doing out here?"

"She ran out and I had to catch her," Stephen calmly said. Kristin just smiled.

After a few minutes I could breathe normally. I gave the police officer my name, thanked him again, took the hands of my children and walked home.

Then I panicked again. I realized I had left my baby alone in the house with the front door unlocked. The three of us ran the rest of the way. I had visions of an officer standing at my door waiting to arrest me for leaving a baby alone in the house. And children on the highway. Roy was sleeping, oblivious to this recent family trauma. I called Bill at work and said, "I CAN'T DO THIS. I NEED HELP."

Evelyn, who had been cleaning house for us since Stephen was born, had retired. I tried to handle the upkeep of house and family. All I could do was cook, keep the kitchen clean and do laundry. I had little time for anything else. I was not the organized household manager I thought I was. Two little red coats convinced me I still needed help.

Fran came to clean house for us soon afterward. She brought her special needs son with her and laid him on the couch during her stay. The little kids played around him and Shane delighted in their antics. He could not speak, but turned his head and smiled as he watched them. My children had an introduction to someone different than them and felt comfortable around him.

Fran was followed by Ann who helped me manage our family of eight into our next home. The daughter of good friends became my "mother's helper" for the little kids during two summers. Hilde, a German woman recommended by a new neighbor, cleaned house for us for the next thirteen years. From our lunchtime discussions, Hilde and I decided to write a book entitled *WHILE* about our contrasting lives during and after WWII. (The book was written after all were out of the house when I had time to write.)

I had more than household help.

Waking with Words

Before I open my eyes I hear
Fast-paced voices announce
The time is
The weather is
The temperature is

I roll over. I hear
A semi overturned
A movie review
An ad for windows
The political news

I throw back covers. I hear
The city's overnight crisis
New and used cars for sale
Celebrities' news
Progress in peace talks

I arise. I hear
The best pizza is
Last night's scores are
The symphony's schedule is
The economy this week is

I silence the radio.
Set the voices
To chatter again
The same time
Tomorrow.

CHAPTER
ELEVEN

And a Railroad, too!

"Want to be a tunnel?" the boys would ask visitors.
"Come to the basement steps and we'll show you how."

They would sit them on certain steps, tell them to
spread their legs, and watch a train come through the
hole in the risers between their feet.

The basement housed a railroad—no earth rumbling, steam spewing giant, but an operating model railroad. Tracks ran around the basement walls, through the steps and hid in shelves, passed over workbenches, disappeared behind the washer and dryer and passed over the laundry tubs.

The HO railroad appeared soon after we bought the house. A full basement was a prerequisite for Bill's hobby. Tracks had to be perfectly level and sit at the same height on all four walls. Creating this height was accomplished during nighttimes after the boys were in bed and out of the way. The procedure involved Bill and me holding a long plastic tube of water and walking around the basement walls. Bill positioned his end of the tube at the height he wanted and marked the wall. I walked around him and held my end against the continuing wall. At the proper level the water in the U-shaped tube leveled out. Bill marked the height for the roadbed where my end of the tube landed. I giggled at this procedure. Several times I commented, "This is such a silly game!"

Bill would respond, "Just wait and see what happens!"

In telling others about the procedure, I found that every engineer knows about using the WATER LEVEL. We walked around the entire perimeter of the basement marking lines on the unfinished walls where the roadbed would lay on a continuous shelf around all the walls. I marveled at what we created and had fun telling others about what I called "water walking."

"Keep the laundry tubs filled," became the kids' every day cry to watch the trains travel over a bridge above the tub of water. Trains ran hidden behind bottles and boxes of laundry supplies and emerged to curve around the tubs and over the laundry basket. This cloth basket hung on a metal frame with wheels. It sat directly beneath the laundry chute from the second floor. It could be added to from the first floor and wheeled over to the washer to unload. I never knew what I would find in it! A banana appeared among the dirty clothes. One of the boys admitted to throwing it down the chute. "I wanted to see if it landed in the basket."

The boys dropped a shoe down the chute and timed how long it took to fall as it clunked down the metal frame. When I asked what they were doing they replied, "Unclogging the sheets stuck in the chute."

I washed clothes every day. The little kids loved to "hepp (help)" with laundry by sitting on the side of the washer and throwing socks and small items in while I dropped in other dirty clothes.

Many days while sorting and washing clothes I wondered about friends who chose a professional life and what they were doing while I was still washing diapers! I experienced my career as a teacher and now saw my career as a mother. Did they?

❖ ❖ ❖

When Lee went to preschool the teacher stated, "Lee likes being on a schedule. He gets upset if we do things out of order." His compulsion came from our routine. After breakfast every day he and I went to the basement to wash clothes. He played while I did laundry. He ran big Tonka trucks around the floor, under the pool table and the workbench. We talked and made up stories.

"Where are you going today?"

"I'm going to Grandma's house," he'd answer. "We're going to bake a cake."

This routine continued with each child when older ones were away at school. Greg always answered, "I'm going to Grandpap's to build a house."

Jay said, "To the airport."

It amazes me that I remember these conversations.

Each child had a small, colored, plastic clothes basket. Bill and I had a large one. I filled the various colored baskets with clean clothes each day. By Saturday the children emptied their baskets in their bedroom drawers and brought them to the basement on Sunday to be filled for the next week.

I was washing dozens of socks got and confused as to whose were whose, so I bought black socks for Lee, blue for Greg and brown for Jay. Later when Lee and Greg went to an all-boys prep school and wore dress shirts and ties, I washed three dress shirts a day, one for each of them and one for Bill.

Men wore suits and ties at the time. I saw my family's outfits, with matching shirts and ties, as a reflection of my job and carefully color coordinated Bill's outfits for the week. He is color-blind and needed to look professional and not wear mismatched clothes. I didn't mind the extra work because if it were up to him, he'd choose whatever was clean whether it matched or not!

❖ ❖ ❖

Many unusual things happened in the basement. Our neighbors to the west had their property sprayed for carpenter ants. Thousands of these creatures crawled over to our basement and died on the railroad! The tracks were covered in a black blanket of carcasses! Bill and the boys spent days sweeping the ants off the tracks with paintbrushes. I couldn't watch the grisly task. I constantly looked for stray ants up in the house and found none. Few things cause me to become unglued. Carpenter ants are one because they are big and crawly and a sign of wet wood somewhere in my house.

Bill's huge built-in workbench sat to the southwest where we hid for tornado warnings. When the sirens sounded, each kid had instructions to grab a necessity before heading downstairs. Lee, the practical one, grabbed the portable radio. Greg, the cautious one, grabbed a flashlight. I grabbed the current baby. Jay, not knowing how long we'd be there, grabbed the cookies. We were set for any emergency.

There were no personal cell phones at the time and Bill's parents in Pennsylvania worried about our living in flatland near the airport. They gave us money to buy a basement wall phone fearing we'd be buried after a tornado with no means of communication. They didn't have tornadoes in Pennsylvania and wanted us to be able to call for help and keep in touch. Usually the sirens wailed when Bill was at work twelve miles away. He would call us to ask how we were. One of us would scramble out from under our hiding place to report our safety under cover. I am still upset with TV stations for airing *The Wizard of Oz* movie in spring, prime tornado season. At every showing I had to reassure the children, "We don't live in Kansas."

The boys' birthday presents were miniature workbenches installed next to Bill's. They built bird houses and anything they could make out of wood scraps. Lee screwed many projects together with what he called "turney nails." Many weekends I would hear uncoordinated pounding from the basement and someone would stumble upstairs holding a mass of wooden shapes nailed together saying, "Look what I built!"

I had to remember to say, "Tell me about it." Many times I couldn't identify the object and didn't want to embarrass myself or the child!

We bought a secondhand pool table for the center of the room. The cue sticks were too big for the boys to use, so the boys would call colors and numbers as they rolled the balls into the pockets. My mother, the teacher, was mortified. "My grandchildren are learning colors and numbers from pool balls?" My dad was happy. His grandchildren were learning a game he loved.

Any child who bounced or threw a ball lost the privilege of playing with pool balls that day. Bill, concerned that I was folding clothes on it and ruining the green baize table top, constructed a wooden cover for the table to be removed whenever anyone wanted to play pool. My mother-in-law, constantly amazed at how much laundry we accumulated each day, teased me by shaking her head and saying, "You'll be folding laundry on your deathbed."

Because of an overhead beam in the basement ceiling, the giant pool table cover could not be raised straight up to be stored. Bill constructed a pulley that allowed the entire cover to rise, turn sideways and be secured above the table.

"Want to see a trick?" the boys would ask a visitor, and pull up the cover and watch it sway into position. Lowered, the wooden cover became the folding table, craft table, Lego and game table.

One year it looked like a boxing ring with string stretched on pegs outlining its top. Wooden clothespin soldiers hung on the string. Their painted uniforms were drying. The pins had been made into Christmas tree ornaments as a money-maker for a craft show! I was in charge of the project and glad to have a space where the project could be painted and dried. Although I felt like a referee, constantly reminding the kids, "Hands off!"

In the winter a swimming pool sat in the corner of the basement. I would buy a twenty-pound sack of rice from the big box store. We would empty the water from the kids' plastic swimming pool, bring it to the basement and fill it with rice. The boys loved running their cars and trucks through the grains. "Watch this," they'd say as a truck ran through a pile of rice. They filled and stacked random sized containers making buildings, played with soldiers on rice hills and in trenches. Summers, the rice went back into the sack, stored for next winter. My children were using their imaginations and I kept up a running conversation to keep them interested.

A boxed-in set of shelves sat at the wall at the entrance to the crawl space on the way down the steps to the basement. I stored canned goods and kitchen supplies there. In our early married years, we had little money and made fruitcakes as Christmas gifts. Every year the cost of the ingredients increased, but we had started a tradition not to be forgotten. One year I stored the ingredients on those shelves. As I gathered them to bake the cake, the ingredients trailed me up the stairs. I noticed a small hole in each of the bags and boxes. A mouse had eaten through into the raisins, nuts and dried fruit.

Our fruitcake was doubly expensive that year! I had to buy replacement ingredients. I was so angry! How dare that mouse! We set a trap immediately and caught him. I am usually squeamish around dead animals, but I wanted to see how fat this mouse was from eating my supplies. The fruitcake has a secret ingredient that is hard to find. Many years I spent hours on the phone calling pharmacies and health food stores to locate it. I have since found the ingredient at a specialty food store. I can't tell the ingredient or my secret will be out, but it does add a wonderful taste and helps keep the cakes moist. I don't store ingredients in the basement anymore!

There were other sad times in the basement. Early one evening, I found one child hiding under the steps crying because he felt left out. I hugged him and we sat on the floor and talked into darkness. I called upstairs for the family to eat dinner. We would be up later. I listened to my child share his feelings of loneliness, not wanting to break the spell and turn on lights. Hours and many tears later, we agreed we felt better and could go to bed. I didn't sleep that night. I prayed for the wisdom to help him. I can still see myself the next day, leaning on the washer sobbing for the sadness in my child. After many phone calls, I did get him help and he became a happier boy.

The three older boys, when in middle school, played strategy games on the pool table cover. Each boy would invite his friends for a sleepover on a Friday evening to plan and practice their moves. Lee's team came one Friday, Greg's another. One weekend a month the teams played the game together with six to eight boys in the basement.

They would order pizza delivery in the names of their characters. The pizza delivery boy never knew who lived in our house! When they played "War of 1812" the music of the *1812 Overture* blasted from the boom box. When they played jungle games, Jay's character answered the door for the pizza wearing a camp hat. Our basement became the place where boys could "hang-out on weekends." I knew where my boys were and didn't mind their type of fun.

Saturday mornings I would walk through the family room to the kitchen to make coffee and weave my way through the bodies in sleeping bags. One summer I left our bedroom wearing a short nightgown and robe to go downstairs. Bill shouted, "You're not going down there like that. The floor is filled with adolescent hormones!" I returned upstairs and put on jeans to preserve my modesty.

With teenage boys filling our house and the prospect of our younger ones becoming teens, I wished we had a bigger house and could stay in Gahanna.

Years earlier, when these teenagers were preschoolers, we closed up the Heil Drive house and moved away from Gahanna—traveling away from what we knew, and downsizing our lives.

Travel/Change

We move from place to place

We roll over in bed, fly in the air
Walk into a room, ride in a car.
Change location.

We travel in our minds
Across time and space in books
Gain information, change opinions.

We pack suitcases, lunch boxes
Change homes, change jobs
Vacation new places.

What moves us to move?
Friends, family, adventure,
Money, marriage, aging?

Emotions
Beginnings
Endings

Travel transports us
Our choice is
Where.

CHAPTER
TWELVE

Away from Home
"Are we there yet?"

In the summers of 1971 and 1972 we flew to Seattle where Bill's project for Battelle was at the University of Washington.

We were the youngest couple on assignment and tried to make a good impression, but our first actions were to call Poison Control and find a dry cleaner.

On the plane, three-year-old Lee spilled juice on Bill's only suit. The juice slipped from Lee's little hands and splashed over the right side of Bill's jacket and pants. We knew then what one of our first calls would be in the new city.

We could not know we'd have to make a more important call. Greg was nine months and walking. When we arrived at our rental house, he toddled up to the bathtub and ate a small guest bar of soap. I called Poison Control. The doctor assured us our boy would be OK. The soap would act as a laxative and for a few days we could call him "Bubbles."

At that time, Battelle maintained a campus of modern buildings with meeting rooms, offices and apartments spread across several acres. Our home away from home the first year was a rented house at the edge of campus. The next year we lived in a house in town where we could see the imposing snow-capped Mt. Rainier every day.

A bonded babysitter was available. We were hesitant to hire someone we didn't know, but I had to remember she was recommended. We hired her several times as Bill and I attended company and social functions. It was exciting to meet well-known researchers and scientists from around the world.

Household items became our boys' playthings. Only a few favorite toys could be packed for a cross country trip. Lee and Greg loved to play in the small kitchen in our Seattle house. Greg loved to stack and bang together pots and pans. Lee opened lower cabinet doors, grabbed canned goods and rolled them on the floor. "Jump, Mommy, jump," he'd call as I tried to fix a meal. I would get angry with the boys until I realized they were away from home and needed to be near Mommy. Somehow, I managed to stay upright in their "new playroom."

In 1982 we traveled again to Seattle. We drove seven of us to stay with friends in Indianapolis, took a train to Chicago, met other friends there and boarded a train to Seattle. Lee and Greg were teens, Jay was seven, Stephen two and Kristin two months. (The trip was planned before she was born.) Each of us was responsible for two things.

There is a photo of us at the train station—Lee has his suitcase and a diaper bag, Greg a suitcase and a lightweight baby bed, Jay a suitcase and a diaper bag. Bill carries his suitcase and Stephen in a backpack. I carry my suitcase and Kristin in a front pack.

We booked adjoining compartments and set up a lightweight baby bed between rooms. In one side Lee and Greg slept in upper and lower berths. Jay slept on the fold-out-chair bed. In the other side, Bill and I slept in the berths and Stephen slept on a fold-out-chair bed. The sway of the train helped us all sleep well.

We traveled the northern route to Seattle and the southern route back to Chicago. We followed our route on a train map and the boys were as excited as I was to see scenes from geography books come alive. As we traveled out through land and time zones, that Fourth of July we saw the sky continuously exploding in colors from fireworks across two states.

It was easy to travel with a baby as I was nursing her. I can still shut my eyes and see the beauty of moonlight on the water on Coeur du Lac, Idaho as we traveled on a low bridge and glided across what seemed like glass.

No matter how well trips are planned, life intervenes. Jay had poison ivy. He received a shot in Columbus, one in Indianapolis, another in Seattle. An itchy seven-year-old didn't make traveling easy. We were fortunate that Jay made friends with Louis. All the boys remembered him. Louis was a college-age porter who adopted Jay as his helper, which kept his mind off his troubles.

In Seattle, Bill and I took baby Kristin and attended a Marriage Encounter Convention. We had been active in the movement in Ohio and had the opportunity to meet others from many states. We had prearranged for the kids to stay with Seattle friends. For Jay, we left them with a dozen bottles of calamine lotion.

We spent most summer vacations where we met at Edinboro Lake in Pennsylvania. Bill's parents had rented cottages there for summers. We started joining them when Lee was a baby. Eventually Dad built their retirement home at the head of the lake. There, as the family grew, we relaxed in a peaceful place, took boat rides and played on the beach and spent time with grandparents. In one photo, Grandma and five of us are standing in front of a flower clock at Niagara Falls, New York. We had taken a day trip from Edinboro. My trick for keeping track of the family was apparent. We all wore red shirts. Even Grandma!

We made many trips back to our hometown of Aliquippa, Pennsylvania and stayed with my parents. When Lee was little, we traveled at night hoping he would sleep. On one trip he talked the entire trip saying, "Moon, Mommy, moon." He was fascinated by the light he didn't ordinarily see.

On another trip, we gave preschoolers Lee and Greg mini boxes of raisins as snacks. Years later when we traded in the car, the dealer found raisins embedded in the back seats. He glared at us. Obviously he didn't have children.

The older boys remember plastic covers on the car seats, which were hot in summers. The boys called them "thigh burners."

Some springs we spent in Florida with my parents who wintered there. One year we went by "auto train," so we would have our own car. Passengers' cars were loaded onto special train cars and unloaded at destinations. There was always someone onboard to play cards with the boys. Jay was a baby. There was always someone who wanted to hold a baby. At Disneyworld, we stayed at a nearby motel. My mom stayed there with baby Jay during the day while I went to the park with Bill, Lee and Greg and my dad. I would exit the park and go to the motel and nurse Jay, then back to the park to join my family. It was an exhausting time, but I wanted to see the world through my children's eyes. Upon my returns, at the appointed time and place, I could always find my family among the crowds. They wore matching ball caps.

As the kids grew, they had "IN-CAR ONLY" books. The books helped erase the boredom of calling, "Are we there yet?" and kept all quiet for any trip in the car. The kids looked forward to searching Christmas catalogs and circling toys they wanted. The Richard Scarry series of animal storybooks helped them learn to read as well as be entertained. I would hear giggles and the kids saw familiar animals explaining the world of color by Parrot, seasons by Bobby Bear, doctor visits with Nicky Bunny or being a friend with Polite Elephant. In-car books stayed in the car.

No matter how well I planned snacks and stories, the game of listing license plates from every state or playing "I Spy," nothing assured a smooth trip. Someone always yelled, "I get a window seat. He's singing again. Are we there yet?"

Little did we know our future vacations and returns home would be to a new address.

Vacation

Time away, will it ever come?

Planning for the whole family to be together.
Some families have one- or two-week vacations.

We try for one long weekend.

To be by a calm and beautiful lake
  Invites quiet morning walks,
  Encourages watching fishermen
  Entices children to noisily swim in afternoon heat
  Offers evening boat rides, moonlight strolls.
Memories to stay with me throughout the year.

Is it worth it
  To wash pack and load these clothes
  Then do the same several days later?

      It is.

I do it every year for moments away,
  Relaxation,
  Family memories.
I will work hard getting us all away again next year.

Part II
Nob Hill Hanna House

CHAPTER
THIRTEEN

Nob Hill, Snob Hill?

"You bought whose house?"

"It's a perfect fit for your family."

"You deserve it."

"Mom, it looks like a barn."

*"It does not. It's Danish Colonial Revival," I said in
my schoolteacher voice.*

In turn, the boys were teased about moving to Snob Hill.

One unusual fall Sunday in 1987, seven of us were all dressed for church a few minutes early, so we drove around Gahanna looking at new houses.

We mentioned the free time to good friends who misinterpreted our intent and thought we were looking to buy a house for our family. "We have a friend listing a big house," they said. "You should look at it." They gave our names to a friend who had just become a realtor and was selling her large home.

Her rambling ranch didn't suit us. We're two story people. "I'm handling another large house in Gahanna," the realtor said. "The owners are lowering the price. I can make an appointment for you to see it." By this time, the thought of a bigger house was tempting. We agreed to view it.

A clock opened the way for us to buy the house. The story, as we heard it, was that the potential buyer's grandfather clock wouldn't fit where they wanted to place it. They withdrew their bid which opened the sale.

Excitedly, I called Bill at work and asked him to come home early. The realtor had booked us a showing. The owners had built a new home, moved in and were more than ready to sell.

We looked at the house as a family. The three young ones immediately dove onto the beige shag carpet in the empty spacious front room and rolled around on the floor. I grabbed Bill's arm and led him into the next room. "Look, a bay window in a big dining room! I love it." Holding out my arms, I spun around in the huge kitchen. Standing at the island stovetop, I said, "I can see myself cooking here." I walked back and forth in the spacious eating area in front of three large windows. "We all can eat comfortably here." By that time, Bill was exploring the full basement and workshop for his model railroad and a rec room for the pool table.

The older boys liked the five bedrooms and their separate bathroom. Like the former family's only daughter, Kristin could have her own bedroom and called loudly, "And my own bathroom." Bill and I would have a large master suite. It was a perfect Hanna house!

"I can see us living there," I said at dinner back on Heil Drive. I hesitated, not willing to jinx the possibility. "Can we afford it?"

After long hours of figuring and refiguring our finances, talking to the realtor and the bank, the following week we made an offer and said our prayers for its acceptance.

We needed to sell the Heil Drive house to make the finances work! We could stay in Gahanna and be in the same parish. Most of the kids would stay in the same schools.

The next week I saw the wife of the selling family drive down Heil Drive. I waved and tried to read her expression: friendly or not. I told myself, "If she smiles, I guess she accepted our offer. If she does not, we're sunk." She didn't see me.

❖ ❖ ❖

On December 5, 1987 we signed the papers to own the house at the end of Nob Hill Court. The following week, Bill went on a two-week business trip to Japan. Lee was in his second year of college in Pennsylvania. He learned about our move in one regular Sunday night phone call. Greg was a senior in high school in Columbus, Jay in middle school, Stephen and Kristin in elementary school and Roy in preschool.

I couldn't wait to live in another house and make it my own. The boys were teased for moving to Snob Hill. I told them to ignore the comments.

We hired a moving company and friends volunteered to help us move the weekend before Bill left for Japan. The kids and I arranged furniture, linens, toys, food, and clothing—everything into place in the new house. When he returned, Bill had to look for his things since we had put everything away where we thought it should go. He returned from Japan on his birthday, December 18. He experienced his forty-sixth birthday twice; once before and once after crossing the International Date Line.

He told all, "I'm ninety-two years old!"

The next weekend we were welcomed into the neighborhood at a Christmas party given by a couple we knew only by name. We were warmly accepted as we met neighbors and renewed acquaintances from church and the kids' schools. They all said, "We're glad to see children in the neighborhood again." We knew we would certainly change the neighborhood.

One of the first days in the house, I heard the teenage boys yell, "Oh, oh, look what you did." A colorful paneled glass door opened to the sunroom letting light into the family room. The boys were roughhousing near the glass door and knocked it hard enough to shatter one of the colored glass panels.

"Why were you so close to the door?" I shouted at the boys. "Didn't you know that could happen?" After I examined their hands and arms, I ordered them to pick up the shards of glass. Apart from a few cuts on their arms, no one was seriously hurt, but I still added, "You could have slashed your wrists!"

"Sorry," they said, "just wrestling."

"And you didn't think someone would try to get out of a hold?" I ordered the boys to unhinge the door, wrap it in an old blanket and maneuver it into the Suburban. We made an immediate acquaintance of a neighbor when we took the door to his glass shop in Columbus for repairs. He replaced the glass and reinforced the door with a steel crossbar. It took a year and a half for the guilty ones to repay us for the repair.

A huge deck with built-in benches still sits to the west of the sunroom. It's impressive, as one bench is built around a tree. We were told the deck was built over the cement patio to keep the bugs away. I didn't believe it then and still don't.

The deck is surrounded by huge pine trees. The area became a tree farm planted in the 1930s as part of the Civilian Conservation Corps. During WWII, the trees were to be cut for Christmas trees. Due to a shortage of man power, they remained in the straight lines as they were planted. The pines have grown to sixty feet, some nearly one hundred feet tall, many of which we had to remove. Some toppled from old age, others blew over and leaned toward the house.

One afternoon, Kristin and I were on the west side of the house when we heard a tremendous THUD. We screamed and rushed toward each other. We met at the dining room. "Look at that. The tree broke off at the bay window!"

We could see the jagged points of wood. When we were brave enough, we went outside to see it had landed on the roof, snapped off, and slid down the house to stop at the dining room bay window. Every wind storm we still fear we could lose another tree on or near our house.

We soon learned that other living things were attracted to our house.

Whose Clock?

There's a big old clock
In the big old house where Grandma lives.
One day I asked Grandma,
"Why do you have such a big old clock?"

"It's a grandfather clock," Grandma said.
"Not a grandmother clock?" I asked.
"No, a grandfather's clock," Grandma said.
"Tall clocks are grandfather clocks."

"My grandfather's clock?"
"No," Grandma said.
"Your grandfather's clock?" I asked.
"No," Grandma said.

"That's funny," I said.
"You have nobody's grandfather clock."

"It's your grandfather's daddy's clock," Grandma said.
"Grandpa had a daddy?" I asked.
"Sure. Want to see his picture?
You have your great-grandfather's face."

"He was a little boy like me?"
"Yes, here's a picture of him."
I ran to the mirror. I looked at me.
"I do have the same face!"

Maybe someday I'll have the clock
And be the grandfather to tell
Another little boy who looks like me
About his daddy's grandfather clock.

CHAPTER
FOURTEEN

Bee Hive, Bee House

*"Mom, come up here quickly!" Lee and Greg called
from their upstairs bathroom one morning.*

I raced upstairs, fearing I'd see blood.

*Greg met me at the top of the steps. "You won't be-
lieve this!"*

*Lee stood at the bathroom doorway pointing into
the room.*

"Look at the window."

*The windowsill was black with buzzing bees. More
buzzing came from inside the wall.*

We followed the sound downstairs and stepped outside to see a huge
swarm of bees hanging on the wood under the bathroom window. I ran back
inside wondering who to call for help.

I expected the Ohio State University to have an entomology department
and fumbled through the phone book's list of university phone numbers. I
spent the day calling numerous numbers before one person suggested calling

Ohio State Extension Services. That person referred me to beekeepers listed in the Yellow Pages.

"Bees, thousands," I cried to each one called. "On my house."

All said, "You have to get rid of the queen."

"No, YOU have to get rid of the queen," I said.

No one was available that day.

"But you don't understand," I said in desperation. "There are children here!" I don't know why I thought that meant anything to anybody.

By late afternoon, the last beekeeper I called said he lived on our side of town and could stop on his way home from work. Meanwhile, the swarm of bees grew to the shape of a shiny humming football stuck on my house.

When the beekeeper arrived, he was amazed that the bees were on the outside of the house. "The queen must not have gone inside yet," he said.

"But we hear buzzing in the walls," I said, frantically pointing to the side of the house.

He came into the house and listened. "Put towels at the bottom of doors and windows on this side of the house," he instructed. "It keeps the bees from getting inside."

Bill came home early from work. He knew the situation and how upset I was. One of my first frantic phone calls was to him. The kids were fascinated by a beehive on our house. They kept running in and out of the house to look at "the buzzing football." Corralling them, we explained that they couldn't stay and interfere with its removal. We called friends to ask if Kristin, Stephen or Roy could stay overnight with them. Bill grabbed sleeping bags and took the kids to various friends who agreed to "save" them from their home. We were busy getting the kids away from the house and didn't see how the bees were removed.

"I got the swarm with the queen and the remaining bees should leave by morning," the beekeeper said. "I'll stop back on my way to work tomorrow."

Bill and I heard bees all night as we tried to sleep. We could only hug each other for comfort and pray the bees would leave. We imagined bees swarming over us while we slept. We put every towel we owned under doors on the first and second floors on the east side to keep the bees from entering the house. We covered ourselves with blankets, not for warmth, but for protection from errant bees.

Early the next morning, the beekeeper returned. The swarm had vanished. He assured us the queen was gone and everything would be OK. We walked him through the house to check for more buzzing in the walls. There was none.

"You were lucky," he said. "Bees have been known to come through the overhead light fixtures and invade the whole house."

I gasped and collapsed into the nearest chair when I realized my whole house could have been a beehive.

I still get nervous when I see bees near my house and remember the Hanna "bee house." We learned that anything can happen in a cedar house surrounded by woods.

Hummingbird
From Mother to Mother

Tiny mother
Humming to your home
At dizzying pace

Sit

In your teacup nest
Revealing needle-size beak and tail

Sway

On tree branch over our deck
Protected by green leaves

Survey

The world below
Unafraid of our family.

Soft

Breezes carry barbeque smoke upward
You sit undaunted

Silent

Hatching three eggs in a plush bed
Then whir away for gnats and nectar.

Smallest

Of all birds in summer heat
You produce miniature hummers to

Start

Their journeys darting from lilies
to trumpet vines, drinking from feeders.
I am honored you chose
Our home
To be your home.

FIFTEEN

Whooo's there?

"Whooo's there?" I usually shout from the kitchen when someone enters the front door. Grandkids expect this, don't answer and sneak into the room to surprise me.

Others call out their names since I am usually in the kitchen at the back of the house.

Some just say "Me" and I need to remember who was expected.

A glass-covered chandelier lights the front entryway. I love the clear light radiating from the candelabra bulbs. It adds sophistication to the entryway. When I bought the fixture, I overheard an older lady at a nearby counter saying to her friend, "I had one of those. Couldn't keep it clean. Wouldn't buy another."

I thought, "What a grouchy old lady." I became that grouchy old lady. The chandelier is hard to keep clean! Bill agrees with me as he and the taller boys are the only ones who can reach high enough to clean it without standing on a chair.

One of the pieces of slate at the foot of the stairs in the entryway is loose and CLICKS as it wobbles. We never fixed it. Bill and I used to hear the click late at night when someone returned. We would look at the time, roll over and smile. The tile let us know when the kids came in. "How did you know?" they exclaimed.

When Kristin was ready to date, I overheard the older boys threaten her. "When you go on your first date, we'll line up at the front door and crack our knuckles. Your date will have to run the gauntlet." Lee was out of the house by then. Greg was at a nearby college (but would return), and his fraternity brother volunteered to take Lee's place. "If your date doesn't pee when he sees us, we'll allow him to date you."

"M-o-o-m," Kristin pleaded. "I'll never have a date."

The line-up didn't happen, but the older boys who were home did ask a few questions when one boy came to pick up their little sister. Kristin must have warned her date. He did well and Kristin dated him for a year.

I liked the boy until he wanted to choose her prom gown. I told Kristin, "Absolutely not! You are my only daughter and it's MY privilege." Kristin looked gorgeous in a silver sheath gown.

That same boy came to pick her up in the car he was only allowed to drive for proms—his father's vintage Corvette.

Bill was antsy the entire evening. "Do you know how fast that car can go?" he asked me as we watched our daughter climb into the sleek low car.

I had no idea, but Bill did. He prowled around the house like a cat ready to pounce on the phone that might hold the message that the Corvette had crashed. I finally asked neighbors to come over and play cards to distract him while I prayed that our daughter was safe.

At the top of the steps is the Crucifix that follows us from home to home.

Next to it is a poster-size collage of photos from the travels Bill and I have had; standing on the huge staircase of the Grand Ole Opry Hotel in Nashville to standing outside the gate at Windsor Castle in England.

The wallpaper from the landing to the second floor needed to be replaced along those walls. Our friend and handyman, John, set up a board from the floor across to the hall to stand on to strip and re-paper the two-story wall. Roy, a preschooler, sat on the steps and asked, "What are you doing? Can that board hold you? Can I try?" With Roy's constant questioning, I thought the man would quit, but he patiently answered Roy as he neatly matched and hung flowered wallpaper.

"Yes, I have a boy at my house. I live in Gahanna, too. You can help by holding this." He and Roy became good friends. Roy followed John and watched whenever he did other jobs around the house.

"How do you know how to fix that? My dad and I have lots of tools. When will you come back?" I wonder if his interest may have been a fore-shadowing of his abilities as an electrician.

Kristin and I could hear these conversations. We were camped out in her bedroom at the top of the steps. My little girl had many bouts of the flu when younger, but this time, she had pneumonia.

"Another week?" first grader Kristin moaned as she sat in the doctor's office holding Pound Puppy. For six weeks, I took her to the doctor every Monday for blood work.

Kristin and I both cried when he said, "She's not strong enough to go to school." A milkshake on the way home lifted our mood.

Stephen, in third grade, would rush up the steps after school calling, "Mailman!" and deliver her homework every day and take the completed work back the next day. I fell right back into my teaching mode and homeschooled her. She returned to school "on track." We read aloud all the books in the *Little House* series that winter. My philosophy proved true again: "Reading helps everything."

The older boys slept soundly and were hard to get up in the mornings. If they weren't up when their alarm went off, they would hear me yell up from downstairs, "I want to hear feet on the floor."

Sometimes they would thump the floor and stay in bed. I think they threw a book on the floor to pacify me.

My next call was, "I want to hear two feet on the floor and the shower running."

I threatened to get a wind-up Big Ben alarm clock and put it in a tin pie pan outside their door! That was a false threat, but they didn't know I couldn't do it. That alarm would wake up the little kids too! I couldn't cope with all awake at the same time at 7:00 a.m.

From the boys' bedroom, triple windows sat above the sunporch roof. Some days I would find one screen on the roof below. "We came in late," they'd say.

"We were just looking at the stars," after I saw cigarette butts on the rooftop.

"We needed a lot of fresh air," after I noticed windows open and blinds askew. I didn't ask what happened. I didn't want to know. No one was hurt.

Sometimes a mother doesn't need to know.

We live inside and outside of our house.

The Flu

Help me to be patient with the patient, Lord.
    She has the flu
        Again.

I know others in the family will follow.
        We make weekly visits to the doctor
        And pharmacy.

Give me the strength to make one more trip
        Upstairs to the sick room
        And be cheerful.

Help me to remember
        It's not her fault she's sick.
She looks so pitiful.
        My heart melts at her weak smile.

Help me read one more story
        Do one more puzzle
        Give one more bath
        Play paper dolls one more time.

Let me forget my tiredness
        help her.
        And
        It's only noon!

CHAPTER
SIXTEEN

The Front Room

*"This proves we belong here," I told the family as I
stood in the front room and pointed upward.*

*Oak beams lined the ceilings of the downstairs rooms;
a tasteful addition to the décor of the house.*

*The former owners said the beams were rescued from
a barn and hewn to fit each room.*

*The letter "H" is clearly carved in the side of one beam
in the front room. I was shocked when I found it a few
days after our move, and saw it as an omen.*

*"We don't know who carved the letter," I said, "but
it's meant for us."*

The front room/living room is truly a lived-in room. The fireplace across
the front wall became the backdrop for family photos on special occasions.
Someone always calls out, "Smile, this may be our Christmas card." Our
family has grown from the original family of eight standing in a semi-circle
in front of the fireplace, to members seated on a bench in front of the group,
and later to twenty-three seated on the hall steps.

One Thanksgiving, with spouses and grandchildren, three rows of family were photographed. Stephen drew Santa hats on each member, scanned it and that photo did become our Christmas card. We still hear, "He's bumping me. Stand still. SMILE!"

At Christmastime, the fireplace mantel holds a ceramic Nativity scene. My mother painted the original three members of the Holy Family for Bill and me for our first Christmas in 1964. She added members in succeeding years. Twenty delicately painted figurines now portray the Wise Men and their camels, shepherds and their sheep arranged to approach the manger. The Holy Family sits in a balsa wood barn and various farm animals surround it.

One year before Christmas the cleaning lady brought the Christ Child figure to me. "I found this on a bookshelf," she said.

"He belongs there for now," I replied. She stared at it in her hand, looked up at me. "He isn't placed in the manger until Christmas," I said.

She nodded, saying, "Makes sense," and put the painted figure back on the shelf.

Lee, our oldest, checks every year to see if I have placed the Wise Men and camels at the east end of the scene. He corrected me once when he was a child, and every year makes sure I remember their proper position. I am pleased that the arrangement of the Nativity scene is important to him.

Important to me is my annual ritual for packing and unpacking the collection. Each figure is wrapped in tissue paper. I carefully wrap and unwrap the figures nestled in the fifty-year-old shredded paper. I choose a Sunday afternoon when I have time to myself and remember the happenings in our family since I last held the figurines, and know that I will follow the same ritual next year.

❖ ❖ ❖

One large and one small wooden rocking chair grace the east side of the fireplace where the grandchildren and I sit and read to each other. As a former reading teacher I enjoy watching the children progress from listening to me read a whole story, to reading certain words in a story on their own, to their reading one page and I another, and finally the children reading a whole story to me. A basket of books sits near the rockers. It's fun to see what books they choose to read, and hear them read from the same worn pages their parents did: *Curious George*, *Katy and the Big Snow*, and *Flat Stanley*.

Two comfortable matching chairs flank the west side where Bill and I read our books in the late afternoon sun. The soft blue walls and oak beam ceiling lend an informal atmosphere to relaxing and reading. An extra-long couch sits across from the fireplace. Bill, at six-foot-three, tested the length of the couch before we bought it fifty-three years ago. He embarrassed me when he lay on several couches in the furniture store and approved the one couch on which he could stretch full length. This proved to be a needed exercise for more than his comfort as our boys are tall and also need its length.

Following in his father's footsteps many years later, Greg led a test on a mattress in a store. Jay, in his twenties, working and finishing grad school, moved into an apartment and decided to buy a queen-size bed as his birthday present. Brothers and sister and I went with him to a big box store to buy the mattress.

They pulled down mattresses and placed them on the floor. Jay, six-foot-five, lay on them to test their size. Greg, five years older, also six-foot-five, home from Chicago for the weekend, snapped his fingers and called out positions: "Fetal position, on your side, on your back and spread-eagle." Jay demonstrated each pose. The boys were attracting an audience who clapped at each pose. Kristin and I were embarrassed. We left to buy Jay queen-size linens as our birthday presents.

Beside our long couch sat the piano. Stephen and Kristin took piano lessons and practiced on the spinet. Our German exchange student, Anne, played for relaxation and songs I requested; Billy Joel's "Piano Man" and Schumann's "Träumerei." Eventually the piano went to Lee and Eileen and their boys took lessons. I'm glad it is kept in the family and still being played. I was sad to see it leave my house as it was a tangible reminder of my mother and her musical legacy. The bench was full of basic music lesson books and old sheet music. A friend knew our love for music and gave the family a book of classics. Family and friends enjoyed playing the songs included. Not to be forgotten was the two-fingered duet the children and I always played: "Heart and Soul."

Also in the living room, senior portraits hang on the east wall. Each child has a collage of one large and several surrounding photos depicting their high school activities. Lee stands before a bookcase of books, as he worked his high school years in the library. Greg stands leaning on a floodlight from years as stage crew for school theatre productions. Jay smiles in his white uniform holding a sword from his fencing days. Stephen sits in a camp chair surrounded by programs from plays in which he performed. Kristin holds her French horn from years of playing in marching and concert bands. Roy poses in one photo in his Boy Scout uniform wearing his Eagle Scout badge. I am proud of our children and want to display their interests.

For two winters, we hung a red and white banner with a blue star in the front window indicating a family member in the service overseas. Roy, at eighteen, joined the Marines, quietly married his girlfriend, Whitney, and spent two deployments in Iraq.

Those were long winters full of fear. Every day we heard more and more tragic war stories from parts of Iraq, and I wondered where my boy was. I couldn't let underlying fear consume me, so I kept a journal to help calm my fears and wrote in it every day. At night I fell asleep saying prayers for my son in harm's way. Mondays Bill and I joined others at church to say the Rosary for those in the military.

I placed a photo of Roy at the entrance to our street with the words "Pray Him Home." People commented that they were glad to know of his service and were praying for him. I was especially touched when the school bus drivers remembered Roy and left bags of personal items and snacks at our doorstep to send to him and his unit. We saw Roy once from Iraq on Skype. I couldn't speak. I was overwhelmed with joy at seeing him looking well. He thanked us for the weekly letters and packages our family and friends sent. The employees at the Post Office looked for us every week. Roy's unit out of Dayton gave us a list of supplies to send, and Roy distributed them among the Marines in his unit. It felt good to do something tangible from home.

Home. This Dutch Colonial Revival is our home and continues to be thirty years later. I recently heard the statement, "A room is loved when it's lived in." We live in this front room.

Reading with Grandma

We sit and read
You and I
In two rockers
I sit in one reading to you
You sit in the smaller listening to me.

We sit and read
Me in a rocker
You at my side
I choose one book
Then you.

We turn pages
Look at pictures
Find characters
I read one page
Then you.

Never skipping
One word or page
You know every word
Of some stories
I read, then you.

No one knows
What we share:
Animal tales, people stories,
I read one
Then you.

Giggling, guessing
What happens next or
What could be.
What fun we have
Me, then you.

When you grow up
And I am older
And cannot see
I listen while
You read a book to me.

SEVENTEEN

What's for Dinner?

"The dining room table needs to be bigger to hold all of us for Sunday dinners," I said, planning our first meals in the Nob Hill dining room.

"No children's table."

I always sat at the children's table at my grandparents' house. When I was old enough to sit at the adult table, my grandparents were gone. I missed the experience of eating with grown-ups.

Our Sunday tradition continued and the table grew as the family grew. Bill built two extensions to be added when needed. The larger table now seats twelve comfortably.

At this table I learned that my life would change.

In October 1989, my dad was living temporarily in a nursing home in Pennsylvania. I drove back the three and a half hours alternate Friday nights to see him, and stay overnight with my aunt in Aliquippa. Driving east on I-70 was interesting seeing glowing skies from lights of small town football games along my route. I heeded Bill's warning: "Don't stop at rest areas. It's too dangerous to get out of the car in hunting season." I was careful not to drink anything on the trip or stop at a rest area!

In my hometown, I would visit my dad on Saturdays, go to mass on Sundays at my hometown church where Bill and I were married and drive home. I didn't mind the trips. I knew my dad was lonely. We had fun playing gin together and I enjoyed staying overnight with one of my favorite aunts. Sunday afternoon I'd drive back to Gahanna to have Sunday dinner with my family.

One October Sunday after driving back, I was struck speechless while sitting at the dining room table. Our first-born, Lee, announced that he had given his girlfriend, Eileen, the family engagement ring Saturday night. I was shocked, surprised and happy as I sat with my mouth wide open. Everyone in the family knew about the timing of Lee's proposal and enjoyed watching my reaction. Bill's aunt had given Lee the family ring the previous summer when he took Eileen to meet her. I wasn't prepared for the news that Sunday. I was going to be a mother-in-law! I was excited and happy for them.

Lee and Eileen were seniors at OSU. After 1990 spring graduation, Eileen, a biology/zoology major, went to work on a fishing boat out of Alaska. Lee graduated in the fall of 1990 and worked in retail in Columbus. His graduation followed his Grandfather Hanna's graduation from OSU exactly sixty years earlier in 1930. Another Hanna tradition!

Lee and Eileen planned to marry in June 1991. The Wedding Mass would be at our church. Eileen had been attending mass with our family in Gahanna. Her family had moved since she was at OSU and she felt more at home in our church. I was more than pleased that she already felt part of the family.

Lee and I planned the wedding by three-way phone conversations with Eileen's mother in Cleveland, us in Columbus and Eileen in Alaska. Lee and I visited three reception halls, interviewed three photographers, and discussed menus. We tried to get varied prices. We would discuss prices and impressions by phone and make decisions.

As we drove up to one place suggested for the reception, Lee said, "I don't want to even go in there."

I asked, "Why not? This place is really popular." He stopped the car.

"It looks like a funeral home," he said. We did keep our appointment. The manager was helpful, answering our questions about portions of food and wine.

After visiting other places, Lee chose a hotel with adjoining suites where Eileen's parents and grandparents from Cleveland could stay for wedding festivities. The choice of venue and food was perfect. Our Italian friend complimented us on the food, so we knew it was good. The Nuptial Mass presided by the assistant pastor went as planned, BUT…

The new pastor announced that we were not to take group photographs in the sanctuary after the wedding. Bill and I had given Pre-Cana (marriage preparation classes) at our church. We knew formal wedding party and family photos were taken there. The newly assigned pastor, "Didn't want the church used as a photography studio." For weeks we complained to all who would hear us—at work, at poolside, at church.

"Every bride and groom has formal photos with family and the wedding party at the altar." We were heard. One of the heads of a church committee approached us.

"Tell me the time of the wedding and I'll take the pastor out to lunch." We were extremely grateful and we thank this man every time we see him.

The photographer was not used to being barred from church photographs. He waved Lee and Eileen back into the church after mass. "We forgot the wedding candle. Let's go in and get it." He photographed them at the altar.

Meanwhile, guests and family went to the afternoon reception and waited and waited and waited for the bride and groom and wedding party. We were frantic wondering where they were. Bill and Eileen's father made phone calls from the hotel office. This was before cell phones. No one knew where the wedding party was. I asked the wait staff to continue serving hors d'oeuvres. Thankfully the kitchen was prepared and the guests didn't mind waiting. "Maybe they decided not to come," some guests quipped. "They left town for their honeymoon," others added. Another said, "They're having their own party." I ignored their comments. The wedding party arrived an hour late. They had been stuck in traffic because of an accident on the freeway. We were all frustrated and thankful for their appearance. The rest of the reception went well.

Later, when Lee and I went back to the hotel, the manager complimented him. "Not every young man can do what you did. They have little interest in the planning. You knew what you wanted and said so." Lee and I thanked him. I was proud of my son and glad he trusted me to be part of the planning.

Most people told me that as the mother of the groom, "All I had to do was wear beige and show up." I wore a deep purplish red dress.

I laughed, saying, "I did more than show up." People commented that I didn't cry watching my firstborn marry. My reply was, "I was relieved that all our planning fell into place."

Greg's fraternity brothers almost burned down our dining room! One brother didn't have money to take his girl to a restaurant to propose. Greg asked if his fraternity brothers could use our dining room for a formal candlelight dinner. I agreed. "The price is one of your cheesecakes from the menu." The brothers came at 4:00 p.m. with their tuxes and bags of ingredients to make the meal.

Bill and I left the house with Stephen, Kristin and Roy. We took them out for hamburgers and a movie, expecting all to be well when we returned.

The brothers set the table with my good china and silver, tablecloth and cloth napkins and lit candles. The couple came at 6:00 p.m. The brothers in tuxes served them wine and closed the doors to the kitchen to give them privacy. Steve was to give a ring to his girlfriend, Dawn.

The brothers listened at the door. "Oh no!" they heard Steve shout. They thought after all their hard work she had said no. Steve came barreling through the kitchen. "The ring is in the car. It's locked." Sheepishly, he admitted, "The keys are in the car!" The guys called the police and went out to help open the car door. Dawn was left sitting at the dining room table.

A few minutes later, Dawn ran outside shouting, "The ovens are smoking!" Everyone dashed into the house. They tried to use the fire extinguisher and called the fire department. Firefighters came and sprayed the ovens. The white kitchen cabinets, the ovens and the cheesecakes were black.

When we pulled into the garage, we saw Greg hanging on the door frame. His face was streaked in black, his tux shirt rumpled and he looked exhausted. "It's safe to come in now. The police and firemen have just left."

"What?" I screamed. "What have you done?" I clutched my chest as if I'd had a heart attack.

Bill, who shows little emotion, sprang out of the car. "Are you OK?"

"You can't go in the kitchen tonight," Greg said as he directed us to go in the front door. "We haven't finished cleaning." I couldn't imagine what had happened to my kitchen.

He led us into the front room where six guys in dirty tux shirts lay spread-eagle on the furniture. They were exhausted. "We're sorry, Mom. We tried to clean your kitchen before you came, but it needs another round."

I felt sorry for the guys but concerned about damage to my kitchen.

"I hope she said YES after all this," I said, sweeping my eyes around the room.

Bill and Greg went out the next morning and bought coffee and donuts for us and the brothers who came back to scrape black crust from the ovens and restore my grey cabinets to white. The whole experience could have been worse. The kitchen still works and the engaged couple were happy, although they never married.

Stephen also hosted a formal dinner in the dining room. He and his friends didn't have money to go to a fancy restaurant before prom. His friends came with tuxes and lugged bags of ingredients to cook in our kitchen. Stephen arranged a centerpiece of plastic flowers and candles on mirrors extending down the length of the table. Good china and silver were used again.

Bill, Kristin, Roy and I ate in the kitchen.

Suddenly we heard, "FIRE! The flowers are on fire!" I couldn't believe another fire at a dinner in my house! I rushed in to see a line of flames from the shortening candles and melting flowers. The girls were fanning themselves from the heat with their napkins, causing flames to shoot higher. I couldn't find my candle snuffer. (The teens didn't even know what a candle snuffer was.) I ran to the kitchen for baking soda to sprinkle on the melting arrangement and wished the couples a better evening.

After dinner, Bill took photographs of the couples in the side yard. I thought they would remember that night without photographs, but it was prom night and everyone needed photos with their dates. The girls hugged and thanked me as they left. The guys had been to the house before and just yelled, "Thanks again, Mom."

Later we could laugh about the "table of flames," knowing no one was burned and no permanent damage was done to the table.

Often when Bill traveled to Seattle, he brought home a salmon or had one shipped home in a cooler. Couples who knew of his trips waited to hear when he would be home and knew they'd be invited to a salmon dinner. One year the couples arrived and the salmon did not. Frustrated and angry about the delay, Bill called the airport and said, "If you don't deliver the cooler by this evening, you can keep it!" The salmon arrived as we were having cock-tails. Bill and I, our guests and the airline were relieved!

The Seattle salmons were always delivered gutted, but I read instructions to Bill on how to remove the skin from the fillets. The boys stood nearby watching and grabbed the head when we weren't looking. They hid it numerous places in the house. It looked at me from the microwave, from a bathroom sink, and/or from under the morning newspaper.

At another spring formal dinner in our home, Bill and I introduced Greg's fiancée, Nancy, and her parents from Chicago to our Columbus friends. Greg and Nancy had just become engaged and ours was one of many celebrations honoring their love. Later that summer, Bill and I hosted the rehearsal dinner in a club high above Chicago and its nighttime view. Greg and Nancy married in a beautiful old Catholic church on the west side of Chicago. Both families were very proud that the couple included all their brothers and sisters and other family members in the wedding ceremony. An evening dinner and reception with a live band and dancing was held in the elegant Chicago Club. (Bill and I tuned up our dancing with lessons beforehand.) Our friends who attended said "we cleaned up nicely."

In later years, the dining room table was set for various events. On every occasion I was pleased to know our dining room table was used for dining and not piled high with mail, newspapers and magazines as I have seen in other homes.

Holidays/Celebrations

Families, friends gather
Sharing food, conversation.
Aromas of baking and cooking traditional foods
Fill warm kitchens.

Good china and silver re-emerge
To enhance
Plate filling meals.
Stories dance around tables
Teaching young about the old.

Newly stuffed shuffle from their seats,
Leftovers divided,
Faraway loved ones call
Goodbyes said
Memories savored.

When holidays come again
We're ready
To reconnect
To celebrate
To gather

Together.

EIGHTEEN

Room for One More

*"Buy a table and chairs that match," my dad said when
he came to visit us for the first time at Nob Hill Court.*

"My housewarming gift."

We received another housewarming gift from a couple whose husband was from a large family. A dinner bell! It sits on the corner of the kitchen island and is used when all are home or when Bill is working downstairs in his basement workshop or upstairs on the computer. Its ring is better than my yelling. Ringing the bell only once or twice a week now reminds me of earlier times when I rang it three times a day every day to call family from around the house.

Bill sat on the floor to change the electric stovetop to gas. His creativeness and talent led him to eliminate the drop-in electric stovetop and its hood. Our tall boys kept hitting their heads on the overhead hood of the island when hunched over the burners to cook. This caused many cuts and bruises, burned food and unprintable words.

Bill installed overhead can lights in the soffit where the hood had been. He constructed a down-draft from the stovetop through the cabinet, between basement rafters and outside. He sat on the floor making a set of drawings, reconfigured the island's lower shelves and made it happen. Again I marveled at his ability to make such a significant change that worked. The boys teased us. "A crowd of animals will collect at the outside exhaust vent drawn by the aroma of Hanna cooking."

The memory of my mother using an overturned plastic dishpan in the sink with another on top, helping her to stand straight when washing dishes, led us to raise the height of the sink and countertop. We are taller than the previous owners. Solid raspberry-colored tiles were added to mask the gap of the elevated countertop. Two ceramic cookie jars, Puss in Boots and a Gahanna lion, sat again with the statue of the Blessed Mother in the corner of the counter. The statue is still my source of strength. Many times I talk to her saying, "How much do I say without being pushy? Help me understand my children's decisions."

In summer times we keep the kitchen shades raised to enjoy backyard greenery. One of Greg's college friends, Vaz—a Hungarian student—remarked that looking out our windows at the trees surrounding our house reminded him of a "dacha" in his country.

Over the countertops, white wooden cabinets striped with black grooves, barn door-like hinges and black knobs, needed to be changed to a neater look. To avoid the cost of new cabinets, Bill set up a five-stage operation in the garage to clean and sand, repaint and replace hardware. He painted doors off-white and repositioned hinges and replaced knobs to brushed nickel. Adding under-cabinet lights lit the workspace. One friend commented upon entering the kitchen, "The room has a wonderful uncluttered look!" Another said, "I'd kill for this kitchen."

A friend gave a demonstration of kitchen products for a bridal shower on our stovetop. Bill made a whiteboard cover and the representative prepared food with her products, baked them in our ovens and served the food to shower guests who bought products for the bride-to-be. The cover with can lights overhead made my kitchen look like a set for a television show!

The cover is also used for added prep and serving space. For Stephen's birthday parties, he requests guests bring/make a pizza as a gift. The display and variety of tastes, from traditional with meats, to desserts with fruits, to refrigerator pizzas with veggies, is amazing. One guest came with a shopping bag full of ingredients. I teased him, "You cleaned out your cupboards for this pizza, didn't you?" Surprisingly, his corn and raisin topping was tasty!

For Stephen's and Kristin's teenage birthday parties, I set up scavenger hunts in the neighborhood. I asked neighbors to participate, cut up two recipes for chocolate cookie pizzas into jigsaw pieces and gave neighbors a part of the recipe. Two teams of birthday guests went to the homes, one team on each side of the street, to ask for a recipe part and bring it back and make the pizza. With double ovens ready to bake, both pizzas could be cooked at the same time. One year Stephen asked his team to bring rollerblades to help his team make the first pizza. Neighbors reported, "We had as much fun as the birthday guests. When's the next party?"

The kitchen is the center of other celebrations for significant milestones. For our twenty-fifth wedding anniversary, caterers prepared and served a buffet dinner. The food was attractively arranged in the living room and guests ate at tables in the kitchen, dining room, family room and cleaned-out garage. Heavy rains canceled outside dining plans. Thunderstorms erupted all evening. After guests left, the power went out. We washed dishes by the light of a candelabra! We were teased for being like Liberace and his candelabra. I hoped the continuous storm wasn't an omen for a stormy marriage to follow. It was not.

After Sunday mass and a blessing, and photos with the family, we celebrated our fiftieth in our home. Each downstairs room had a table with food and a poster with photos from one decade of our marriage. The weather was beautiful, and after getting food from inside, guests ate on the deck and under a spacious tent in the yard. Outside, guests met our family. Many friends had not seen our children as adults, nor seen our grandchildren who ranged from eighteen months to sixteen years with two more grandsons on the way. Our most heard comment was, "You haven't changed a bit." Bill still has a crew cut and wears glasses. I still stand as tall as his chin, but I've changed. I have white hair!

There is always room for one or two or more at our table. One winter when the electricity went out for days because of an ice storm, on the first night, we invited the neighbors in for chili while they made arrangements to stay at nearby hotels. Fifteen people sat at the kitchen table booking reservations from their cell phones. We had heat and light because we had a natural gas generator Bill designed and was testing for commercialization. Our family was comfortable with heat, refrigeration, and some lights for five days. We were "neighborhood central" as neighbors called in from their hotels each day to ask if electricity had been restored.

Holiday dinner preparations changed in my kitchen. As the children became older, they prepared parts of the holiday meals. I am glad for my family's help, but their jobs leave me a spectator in my own kitchen. For many years as I stood at the kitchen sink peeling potatoes, I wondered how many other mothers were making the same preparations at their sinks. I always felt connected to them through this ritual.

I bake pies on football Saturdays. Few in the family like Ohio State football as much as I do. They leave me alone in the kitchen to mix dough from my mother's recipe, roll out dough with my mother's rolling pin and bake pies while watching football. My family loves fruit pies. I continue to add double fillings: no "meet pies." The boys' friends remember my pies, and when in town, they stick their heads in my kitchen saying, "It's a football Saturday, Mrs. H. Are you baking pies?"

The family meets every fall for apple picking at Lynd Fruit Farm, an orchard thirty minutes away. I love these days. Each year a new generation rides on older shoulders to pick apples—a tradition chronicled in photos. Each family buys bags of apples and a jug of cider. All return to our house to pare and core crisp juicy apples for immediate pies. During the next week the house is filled with the smells of cinnamon and cooking applesauce. Remaining apples are sliced and frozen for future pies.

Kristin and Shaun became engaged on one apple picking trip. They began dating in winter after divorces from first marriages. I accepted Kristin's divorce. I didn't want my daughter to be miserable the rest of her life. Shaun was introduced to our family at a picnic in the following summer. He and Kristin came back in the fall for apple picking. When the family had filled their bags with apples, Shaun called all of us around his car, knelt and proposed, presenting Kristin with his grandmother's diamond ring buried in an apple. We were all surprised, except for Bill. Shaun had talked to him the previous night. Photos from that day show Kristin's surprise as she beams, holding up her left hand sporting the ring on her finger.

We always buy a HUGE pumpkin on the way back from the orchard. The strongest son hefts it on his shoulders and puts it in our trunk. Back home, he places it in a wheelbarrow and wheels it to the deck where it's cleaned out. When little, Lee used to say he was scraping "weeds and seeds." Stephen carves the pumpkin into a Jack o' Lantern to sit on the wall in front of the house. He carves an intricate design on the front which glows from its lighted inside. I separate and rinse and dry seeds, coat them with garlic and butter and bake them for a salty snack!

The day after Thanksgiving, Bill and I make the traditional twelve pounds of fruitcake. It takes two of us to stir its ingredients in the roaster pan that baked a turkey in the previous twenty-four hours. Making this cake reminds us that the holiday season begins. The three cakes bake all day, are brushed with liquor, and sit for three weeks until opened on Christmas Eve. Certain friends look forward to slices of the moist brown fruity cake and never guess the secret ingredient which keeps it soft and moist. Our fruitcake is not the hard cake depicted as a doorstop!

The January after waiting a year from "the apple orchard engagement," Kristin and Shaun were married in a civil ceremony in Perrysburg, Ohio. Bill and I, Lee and Will, Jay and Stephen attended the ceremony along with Shaun's father and his wife. Kristin carried five red roses, one for each of her five brothers. Shaun's children—Olivia, nine, and Owen, six—stood as their attendants. The ceremony, presided by a judge, was plain, but meaningful. It changed my perception of weddings. I realized a couple doesn't need a big wedding party, months of planning and huge expenses to make it real or legal. We went to a park along the river for photos and then to a restaurant for a celebration hosted by Shaun's father. We were happy for the newlyweds. They were happy again. My Catholic faith still wanted the blessing of the Church, but this was my adult daughter's decision and I respected it.

High chairs, youth chairs and folding chairs are a never-ending part of our expanding family.

When we moved to Nob Hill Court, Roy sat at the table in a youth chair. Now his children sit in the same chair. When others left for college, or "out on their own," fewer chairs lined the table and the leaves were stored. It makes me sad to adjust to the diminishing number at the table and learn to cook for fewer people. I laughed when out of habit, I set out three of every portion after Stephen, Kristin and Roy left home. They were so close in age, I did everything in threes: i.e. three place settings, three milks, three child servings. Bill teases me, "You are most happy when any member of the family comes back." He's right! I enjoy seeing and hearing the banter between my children.

A measuring wall stands in the hallway where we mark the growth of our kids and grandkids. This wall will not be repainted and will continue to be marked as the children grow. Greg and Jay top the chart at six feet and five inches. The grandkids love to be measured each birthday and compare their height with others at the same age. "Stand flat," they say. "No tip toes."

The kitchen is the hub of the house from the first cup of coffee in the morning to the running of the dishwasher at night. Its ebb and flow follows family changes.

Kitchen Table/Family Friend

I am an American institution without walls,
Always big enough to seat one more person.

I encourage people to sit, talk and listen
To linger and enjoy kitchen life.

I collect things for families
Daily newspapers, lists and notes, folded napkins.

I provide a large working space
For cutting out cookies, printing posters, opening maps.

I educate people from table talk
Of homework, daily and world news, observations.

I offer stability to a household in turmoil
Arguments and tears, hugs and smiles.

I stimulate after-dinner discussions
Recipes for gravy, family stories, political debates.

I display celebration cakes and gifts,
Funeral meals, holiday buffets and potluck suppers.

I hold stains of blueberry and ink, scratches from knives,
Hot mugs' white rings, dulled finish from spills; signs of my history.

I nourish the world with feasts of food, words, and family time.
I must not be replaced with a breakfast bar.

I am the family's friend, an American institution.

NINETEEN

Put a Sock in It

"What are these red things on my socks?"

"There are strings on my jeans."

I heard these complaints after someone decided the Raggedy Andy doll needed cleaned.

For the next week we all wore a bit of Raggedy Andy.

Between the kitchen and TV room is one of the most important rooms in the house—the laundry room, not my favorite room. Our washer and dryer fit between the washtub and a hallway door. We didn't need new appliances, but we saw elevated dryers in ads. I wanted mine elevated for easier loading and unloading. "I can do that!" Bill said and built a large drawer on rollers to fit under our dryer.

I am happy to have a first-floor laundry room, which eliminates going up and down steps for clean clothes. The laundry room is also a pass-way to the deck. The door to the deck has to be kept closed as animals have been known to wander in for a visit.

Our children and grandchildren love to "hepp" wash clothes. The little ones of this generation sit on the side and drop socks and small items into the washer as did their parents. As a toddler, Roy liked to sit in the laundry chute over the sink and lean over to peer at clothes swishing in the washer as he moved his wrist back and forth imitating the agitator.

As I was throwing clothes down the chute from the second floor one day, I saw the diamond from my engagement ring catch on a piece of the metal frame and fly into a pile of clothes stuck in the chute. I couldn't stretch my arm far enough into the chute to free it. I ran downstairs screaming, "NO-BODY MOVE!"

I was so thankful the kids listened to me that time and stopped where they were! When I couldn't reach up for the bundle from the laundry room, I called for three-year-old Roy to crawl in the chute. "Pull everything down carefully."

We slowly pawed through the clothes as they fell. We found the diamond stuck in a shirt buttonhole. For many years, Roy pulled visitors into the laundry room and told his "Hero story" and demonstrated how he rescued Mom's diamond.

Collections of family photos hang on the laundry room walls and keep me laughing while I do the unending chore. Photos show Stephen sitting in a dryer, clutching his knees and smiling through the circular window. Kristin's smiling face and two side ponytails can be seen popping out of the washer as a brother playfully stuffs her into the machine. Roy grins from the open door of the chute.

The laundry room became a bar for Greg and Nancy's engagement party. With a shelf to span the doorway, Stephen mixed drinks from the supply of liquor on the washer and dryer and cold drinks from the ice-filled laundry tub. That tub has held ice and bottled drinks for many parties. It is an ideal location since it's easy to pick up a cold drink on the way out to eat on the deck.

The overhead cabinets above the washer and dryer hold odds and ends of cleaning supplies, tins for cookies, paper plates and candy. I buy Halloween candies in October with each week's groceries and hide them behind the odds and ends in these cupboards. The bags' candies disappear as the holidays approach. For years I accused the kids of eating the stash. Now the candy supply diminishes and the kids are gone! The kids were not the only thieves. Bill always found the candy too!

Seeing the family photos in framed collections help make wash days pleasant. While scrubbing out stains I see Bill taking the license plate off the Suburban to donate it. His body is slumped, his head is down. The Suburban began growling on one trip to visit Kristin in college in Toledo. Bill took it to a shop where he was told it was too costly to repair. He was extremely frustrated. He had just bought four new tires, which now had to be given away with the vehicle. This big Suburban that hauled our family and groceries, scouts and lumber, kids to college and furniture and appliances, was left in Toledo. We said goodbye to our well-used vehicle and signed it over to Goodwill, and drove home in a rental car.

While cleaning lint out of the dryer screen, I look up to see us happily dancing at weddings, sailing in Tahoe with friends, sitting at a reception after Bill won an award. While hanging shirts on hangers, I see Lee's family smiling from Will's Confirmation ceremony, Greg and Nancy's first dance after their wedding, Roy and family gathered on our front lawn, Jay and Stephen innocently smiling after their dinner table antics, Kristin and family sitting on a park bench after our outing with them. I remember these times and am filled with love for my family and continue folding clothes.

Across from the laundry room door is a professional photograph of a mature maple tree exploding with red leaves. The photographer shot midway up the thick black trunk and captured multiple limbs holding clusters of deep fall reds. Glimpses of bright sunshine appear between wide maple leaves. I feel embraced in its towering presence. It reminds me of the tree outside my mother's second floor bedroom window. When abed with debilitating migraine headaches, she always said, "Looking at the tree remaining strong throughout its seasons gives me strength to endure." I am reminded of that strength when I see the photograph and it gives me strength.

The laundry room will continue to be a laundry room. Nothing can replace its function to a household, but it can become a pleasant place because of the memories I see there.

Stately Tree

My backyard tree stands majestically stilled; a stag, a hart
        Trunk curves for neck and back.
        Thick body supports a playhouse
        Antler branches hold squealing children.
        Limbs sway with birds and squirrels.

Leaves mingle with neighboring trees
        Form a green awning, shade my yard
        Shelter bird and animal families.
        Changed by years of seasons
        The weathered giant remains erect.

Over time
        Playhouse rotted into dirt.
        Children no longer climbed.
        Birds and squirrels played in new trees.
        Aging branches snapped.
        Yet this black-barked tree stands alert.

Continues
        Serving, shading, supporting
        Reaching upward, reminding me
        I have weathered changes
        Strengthened, I hold my head upward
        Facing changes in my life.

CHAPTER
TWENTY

Remote Please!

"My turn, not yours. Get away from me. I was here first."

"Mo-o-m, he's hiding the remote. I don't want to watch his show."

"She's hogging the recliner again. I want to sit there."

Then I'd hear the THUNK and a giggle as the chair tilted backward.

TV dominated our family room.

We moved into the 21st century a few years ago. Between two windows on the front wall hangs a fifty-two-inch screen TV where the Christmas tree always stood. Greg offered the TV when he upgraded his set, IF we could get it in the car to bring home from his home in Chicago. I stated, "We will fit it in the car if I have to give up my seat and fly home." I hate to fly. We made the flat screen fit in the car and at home.

An 8x12 foot National Geographic map of the world, mounted and left by previous owners, covers half of one wall. Plastic colored stick pins indicate travels of our immediate family and foreign exchange students. Pins are scattered over the map. From Roy's military missions to Norway and Iraq,

Bill's business trips to Japan, and homelands of ten exchange students, fifty pins dot the map. I am glad to explain the map and its pins to those who ask and to grandchildren who are learning places in the world.

Four bookshelves face the map and hold collections of books and toys. One of the exchange students asked as he first entered the room, "Have you read all of these books?" to which I nodded.

He shook his head. "I can't believe you own so many books!" I didn't tell him of our weekly trips to the library to borrow other books, which added to those we read.

Toys for the grandchildren sit on the bottom shelves of two bookshelves. Most were their parents' toys. Colors may be faded, but the barn door continues to "moo" when opened, the parking garage elevator cranks up and down and pings and the village still houses people and stores. I love to hear "vroom, vroom" as a grandson crawls on the floor and pushes a car, or a granddaughter sings "Twinkle, Twinkle, Little Star" while riding on a rocking horse, and another rearranges a transformer into its many shapes.

Atop one bookshelf sits a prize possession—my great-grandfather's fiddle and its bow grace the shelf. The fiddle was made from three types of wood from Pennsylvania forests. William Lytle Craig played for barn dances on the farms around the western part of the state. I often wonder if my mother's talent for playing the violin came from him. She played violin at an early age and told of being taken as a teen to Indiana to have a violin made for her. She continued to play and teach music through most of her life. I did not inherit her ability to play, but have an appreciation for good music. Stephen now plays his grandmother's restored violin.

Another family possession hangs on the opposite wall: a long percussion cap .25 caliber squirrel rifle. It belonged to Bill's great-grandfather who used it as a hunting rifle in the woods of eastern Pennsylvania. "The rifle was taken in trade from a local doctor who shot small game from horseback," Bill said in explaining it to the boys who tried to hold the heavy object. I display these inherited possessions in the family room to tell their stories and teach the kids about their ancestors.

A recliner chair faces the TV. Another recliner became my "bed" when recovering from shoulder surgery. Friends lent us their electric recliner. Bill and Jay loaded it onto a truck and brought it to our house. The handle to position the seat was on the right side and I could not reach with my right hand in a sling. Bill ran cords under the chair so I could make adjustments with my left hand. I laughed with the grandkids as they called it "Grandma's electric chair." They could sit in it, lie in it and send themselves forward into standing just like Grandma.

Family fills the room to watch movies. *Flubber* is a favorite of the grandsons. The granddaughters like *Corduroy*. If their grades were good, our kids were allowed to stay up one night a week to watch a favorite show. Stephen watched *Are You Being Served?* Kristin and exchange student Anne from Germany liked the movies *Clue* and *Pride and Prejudice*. Anne-Laure from France liked *Dracula*, and Leo—an exchange student from Venezuela— liked Oliver Stone's version of the Kennedy assassination.

All the kids loved *True Lies*. I caught snatches of scenes and made the comment, "I can't believe that!" Every time they viewed the movie, they called me in to catch certain scenes and hear my comments. "That wouldn't happen! How can you watch this?" It became a game to "Watch Mom Watch the Movie." This big room has held many parties as well as family TV viewing. Wedding showers and anniversary dinners, book discussion circles and card club. Teens sitting on the floor playing card games and Monopoly have filled this room with love and laughter.

Our family room, TV room, whatever it's called, is constantly in use since it has the door for our entry and exit to and from the garage. It leads us to where we're going and brings us home.

Conversation with a TV remote

Why don't you do what I want?
>You're going too fast. Slow down.

I'm following directions.
>No you're not. Give me a chance to do what you ask.

Others get what they want from you. Why can't I?
>Look what you're doing.

I'm pushing the right buttons.
>But you either go too fast or too slow.

No, I don't.
>Yes you do.

You go where you want.
>Yelling at me won't help.

But you don't listen.
>I can't hear you!

I'm ready to throw you at the screen.
>Go ahead. That won't help you get the right channel.

TWENTY-ONE

Visitors

"My grandma told me you had grandsons," the five-year-old said, standing in the doorway. Her grandmother and I were seated at the glass table in our sunroom.

I nodded. "I do."

Hands on hips, she said, "Then what is this kitchen stuff doing here?"

I calmly replied, "My grandsons play restaurant with it."

"OK, then." She stepped into the room and began playing in the miniature kitchen.

Kristin's former play kitchen has become a permanent fixture in the sunroom. Grandson Thomas used the plastic blender and made imaginary "tomato milkshakes." I clicked my tongue and pretended to drink this concoction. Will, his brother, carefully wrote menus and bills for the imaginary food served.

Later years little granddaughters served their creations in that kitchen at just their height. "Cranberry pie, Grandma. No ice-cream today." I licked my lips, pretended to taste the tart cranberries and asked for a cup of coffee.

Our sunroom sits behind the TV room. The bright white room with fourteen windows gives a panoramic view of the wooded lot behind the house. The cedar beams throughout the house are repeated in the trim of this room addition. From our seats at the table or seated on the small couch, we watch the seasons appear as snow settles on pine trees, green leaves screen neighbors' yards, birds flitter from branch to branch, squirrels scamper from tree to tree and occasionally deer roam through the yard.

We designated the sunroom to be my dad's bedroom when he, at eighty-two, came to have open heart surgery and recuperate with us. There is a half bath on the same floor and his only complaint was, "I hate taking bird baths in the little sink."

Dad had a bed, dresser, recliner, TV and table and chairs in his own space. He and the older boys watched baseball games and played many games of poker and gin in that room. He was cajoled into reading stories to the younger ones. I laughed to see him draw stick figure cartoons and speak for them as he did for me when I was at each of their ages. They sat and laughed as he incorporated what happened in the house into his cartoons. I was glad I could monitor his diet and recovery within my family setting.

The first day Dad came was disastrous. A friend stopped by to say hello. They were sitting calmly talking when four-year-old Roy ran into the room, his face covered in blood. He and Kristin were building rooms up in the playhouse out in the yard. He was calm, but Kristin was hysterical. I shouted, "What happened?"

"A brick dropped on me," Roy said.

Kristin cried, "It was an accident. I didn't mean to drop it."

Dad clutched his chest and went pale. I thought he'd have another heart attack.

My mother-mode kicked in. I grabbed Roy, cleaned him up, handed him an ice pack and called Bill to meet us at Children's Hospital. I asked my friend to stay with Kristin and my dad.

I slung my purse over my shoulder, picked up Roy clutching the ice pack on his forehead and jumped in the car. We met Bill in the emergency room at the hospital, registered and were tended to right away. A doctor came into the examining room to stitch Roy's forehead. Bill asked him how many of these he did a day and he answered, "That's all I do!" Roy needed five stitches inside and four outside. I held my son's hand. Mine was shaking. I prayed to stay strong. My strength was fading in the excitement of handling the situations with my dad and my son.

My dad's stay was a good summer for the family. Dad and his grand-children reconnected. When he thought the three younger ones too noisy, he would shut his door for privacy. He saw Greg graduate from high school, continue to work at Bob Evans restaurant and be accepted at Capital University. He saw Lee complete his second year of college in Pennsylvania and return home to finish at The Ohio State University.

Dad recuperated quickly from a quintuple bypass in May and returned home in the fall. We missed him, but knew my aunt was keeping an eye on him and she kept us posted on his progress. Dad returned two years later to live in our sunroom again as his health was failing. Roy was in afternoon kindergarten. I would put him on the bus and jump in the car, visit my dad in the hospital and be back home when the older kids came home from school.

One day I was so tired I couldn't remember what floor of the parking garage I had parked on and had to ask for help to find my car. My friend Jo who worked near the hospital volunteered to visit my dad on her lunch hours so I could visit him every other day. They became good friends as both were interested in numbers; Jo an accountant and my dad a banker. Dad died of pneumonia after six weeks in the hospital. He wanted to see "big city doctors, sell his house and see the grandchildren" before he died. He did all three. The sunroom was no longer his but his spirit is still there whenever we play cards in the room.

One August evening around 10:00 p.m., alone in the house, I sat on the couch in the family room watching TV. I heard scratching on wood behind me. Curious, I got up and walked toward the noise and saw black and white fur spread over the doorsill to the sunroom. A skunk! Although I was scared, I knew not to scare the animal. I began to shake, thinking of the possibility of the skunk stinking up my house. I quietly said a prayer to calm myself and started to shoo it into the sunroom where I could shut the door and isolate it there. The animal did roll down the step. I slowly closed the door and ran to the kitchen, grabbed the phone book and called the first twenty-four-hour animal removal company I could find. I woke a man by screaming into the phone, "There's a skunk!"

"Where?" the groggy voice asked.

"In my house," I yelled.

"Do you want me to come now?"

"YES," I screamed.

The man sounded more alert, probably from my screaming. "Is there an outside door from the room?"

"NO," I screamed.

"Is there furniture in the room?"

"YES," I screamed again. All I could think of is that we'd have to get rid of everything in the room if the skunk sprayed his scent.

Meanwhile, Bill and Stephen came home. I called them en route. Stephen read from his phone. "Skunks are nocturnal and will spray only if in danger."

A few hours later, the animal removal man came, and with a small flashlight located the skunk scratching at a window screen trying to get out. "That's a big one," he said. "Probably a mamma. Turn out all the lights and stay in one place." Bill, Stephen and I huddled in the kitchen. After two attempts in complete darkness, the man lured the skunk into a trap. He removed it from the house in a large garbage bag without any harm to the animal or the room. No odor. I apologized for screaming at the man on the phone and he understood my hysterics.

The skunk probably entered the house through the open laundry room door. I served dessert to my book club on the deck the night before. Members were coming and going through the door to the deck. The skunk must have snuck in and slept in the potted plants in the sunroom during the day. Since then, the laundry room door and the potted plants are closely watched when anyone goes inside or outside from the deck.

We eat breakfast and lunch in the sunroom when the weather is nice. Drinking coffee and reading the newspaper in the warmth of the rising sun is a great way to start the day. The glass table in the center of the room reflects the trees in seasons outside. A yellow "pineapple shaped" ceramic stove sits in one corner to heat the room. Its wood burning heat creates a cozy atmosphere for reading, playing cards or relaxing on winter days. A love seat sits on the east side—a perfect place for reading. The glass table has led to fun times for playing games with grandchildren, doing crossword puzzles in its sunshine and/or eating meals.

When our grandson Will and I were playing double solitaire, his brother Thomas circled the table, bent over, and looking up at the turned down cards from under the glass he said, "Will, wanna know what your next card is?"

Remembering a neighbor's display of pottery in an open cabinet, I took doors off Kristin's white wardrobe cupboard and now display pottery painted by my mother. In her later years she enjoyed painting molds of cantaloupe and pineapple and their accompanying leaves to be used as attractive bowls for serving fruit. Four sets of these, as well as a tall, red hot chocolate pot and accompanying cups, orange and apple shaped tea cups and plates painted with colorful birds give color to the room.

When we moved our Christmas tree and trains from the family room into the sunroom, we relocated bookshelves, potted plants and the play kitchen for this annual display. The sunroom became the tree and trains' private room at Christmas time. We continue to hold a New Year's Day Open House to entertain friends and families with our display of a small town of buildings with lighted windows. Many bring grandchildren who see operating trains for the first time. I love hearing their "oohs and aahs" as they watch the operating milk car spit out miniature milk cans, log loader send logs up the conveyer belt and oil rig pump imaginary oil.

The sunroom is truly a well-used bright spot in our house year round. Its sunshine in spring and summer brightens my days. Its views of snow-topped pine boughs and the autumn leaves of oaks and maples color my world.

In My Woods

Summer's sunshine splashes backyard trees.
Patches of light create neon greens.
Swaying leaves dance from towering trunks.

Surrounded in an array of stoplight green ash,
Yellow-green elms, pea green oaks and dark green pines,
All contrast with scarlet cardinals perched on limbs.

Brilliant bluebirds hop below,
Yellow finches and black and grey nuthatches climb tree trunks
Adding color to my woods.

My mood is brightened
As I watch from
My aptly named
Sunroom.

CHAPTER

TWENTY-TWO

More Visitors/Exchanges

"I'll pray for you every day," I said, hugging Jay tightly.

"I figured you would," he smiled as he replied. My son turned and boarded the plane that would take him to Germany as an exchange student.

I am afraid to fly, so I began praying as the plane left the runway. "Dear God, take care of my son and bring him back safely."

When Jay graduated from high school in 1993 and was accepted in a nearby college, he was encouraged by his best friends to enroll in the Rotary Foreign Student Exchange Program. Jay was accepted and enrolled to go to Germany. He had studied German in school, saw an opening for that country, and decided to take the opportunity and wait a year for college.

He was to fly to Chicago, meet others from across the country going to Frankfurt, Germany, and then head on to Hamburg where he would meet his host father and brother who would drive him north to their home in Ostseebad Kühlungsborn, a resort town on the Baltic Sea. Jay, at 6'5", was the first American the townspeople saw and they asked, "Are all Americans as tall as you?"

At the time *Les Misérables* was a popular play and I couldn't listen to the song "Bring Him Home" without tearing up thinking of my son and bringing him home. Jay spent a year going to school and living with his host family. His host father was strict. Jay's escape from the household came in visiting his American friend in the neighboring town and swimming with the life-guards in the town pool.

We corresponded weekly. I wrote to him Sunday evenings. Family members here for Sunday dinners added to my letters. In an early letter Jay wrote, "I need a winter coat."

I was confused and replied, "We sent you with one."

He wrote, "I have a down jacket. It's cold here from winds off the Baltic Sea. I need a long coat." We sent him money, and one weekend his host father drove him to the nearest city to buy a three-quarter length coat. He sent a photo of himself wearing a long coat and wrote on the back, "This is what I needed."

The following spring, Bill and I visited Jay in Germany. We were told not to visit until near the end of his stay so he wouldn't be homesick and want to come back with us. I realized how scared he must have been to travel alone when it took us three planes and two trains to reach him. He had always traveled with family and only in the States.

Our trip was after the Wall came down and the Reunification of Germany. We traveled to Berlin from Kühlungsborn and could see the difference between the stark landscape and buildings of the East and lush green and beautiful buildings of West Germany. Arrangements had been made for us to stay in a bed and breakfast in Berlin. We arrived late at night and the place was closed. The owners wouldn't let us in.

We were stranded on the sidewalk with our bags. A mother and daughter walked near us. Jay asked for help in German. The girl answered in English. She had just spent the summer working in Disneyworld and spoke fluent

English. She and her mother knew of a hotel nearby and helped us reserve a room for two nights. The second night Jay and the girl went out on a date.

This was Kristin's thirteenth birthday. She was looking forward to turning into a teen and was angry at us for being away for her momentous day. She was on a Girl Scout overnight in Ohio. We had planned with the scout leader to have a cake delivered to their cabin and arranged for a clown to lead a party. We knew Kristin would have a celebration. We wouldn't forget our daughter's birthday.

That same trip I missed seeing a German friend I had met in Ohio. We agreed to meet for coffee while Bill and I were in Berlin. I thought coffee would be at ten in the morning. Coffee to a German is five in the afternoon. Our train left at noon and we missed seeing each other. I was disappointed and mad at myself for not knowing the cultural differences. I didn't know when we'd see each other again.

Jay traveled south with us through Germany and France. He spoke the language and got us around. We tried to find my Leis ancestors in the Baden-Baden area, but the courthouse and records from their town were destroyed in the war. It was disappointing to be so close and have no more information than when we came. We enjoyed traveling through both countries by train, seeing the Dijon fields of yellow mustard and quaint towns and farms along the route. We heard on this trip that President Nixon had died. It seemed strange to hear the commentaries about his life from another country's viewpoint. He was not seen as disgraced, but praised for his relations with China.

While Jay was in Germany, we hosted Anne-Laure from France in our home. She gave us a view of what Jay must have experienced in his host home.

Anne-Laure was delightful. On one of her first days with us, we took a walk and I asked if she'd feel comfortable calling me Mom. She didn't hesitate. "Of course," she said. "You are my Ohio mom."

Early in her stay, Anne-Laure asked, "Why does everyone stand up each morning in school and talk to the wall?"

Confused for a moment and trying not to laugh, I answered, "They're saying the Pledge of Allegiance to the American flag."

A family in our neighborhood hosted Lone, a Danish student, at the same time. The girls became good friends spending time at each other's host homes. Both spoke English well. Anne-Laure came running into the kitchen one morning beaming. "I dreamt in English!" This was a good sign that she was adjusting well to our language.

I bought tickets for the final summer run of the historical outdoor drama "Tecumseh," thinking I would show the girls an exciting evening of live entertainment in the hills of Ohio. I didn't realize that they didn't know this part of American history. Stephen, who was taking American History at the time, told them what was going on throughout the play.

We invited Anne-Laure's family to spend an American Christmas with us. They landed in the States in Chicago, thinking they could drive a few hours to Columbus. At that time, it was an eight hour drive. I can still see Anne-Laure perched on our chair by the front window watching for her mother and father, sister and brother. They arrived early in the next morning, said hellos and immediately went to bed.

Her family was astonished at the amount of outdoor lights Americans display. Santa brought me a bread maker that year. The French love bread and ate a loaf every meal. They teased me about serving them "electric bread," not loaves from the oven. "We cannot believe this modern invention."

We kept in touch with Anne-Laure's family and visited them on our trip to see Jay in Germany.

Upon leaving Europe, we said goodbye to Jay knowing he would be going on a tour of Germany with other Rotary students and then home. He came home a mature young man knowing he could face anything after a year on his own. When he did go to college, he stayed in a dorm for two years saying, "The students were so juvenile." He felt older and wiser and lived on his own until he graduated.

Lone, from Denmark, came to stay with us when Anne-Laure moved to her second home. Lone was quiet. I could understand that she probably felt homesick for her first host family. We did things differently, which was the purpose of the moves. I was a stay-at-home mom while both parents worked in her first home. Rotary students stay with host families for four months, three months and three months.

Lone was assigned to study the state of Arkansas as a school project. She needed to know current costs of living in the state. Our former Heil Drive neighbors had just moved there. We set up a phone call to them. They were helpful and invited her to visit. Lone asked, "Could we go there?" She couldn't believe what the trip would involve.

I explained, "We would be gone a week—two days to get there, two days to stay, and two days to drive home." Most of the exchange students, including Lone, were from countries with rail service that took them from one country to another in a few hours of travel. Lone learned the vastness of our country when she traveled with all the Rotary students on a later tour of the States.

Inake from Spain lived with us for a few weeks one summer. He was part of an independent program with a group of students to be immersed in American life. Inake experienced living in the city with our family and in the country with another.

Leo from Venezuela was politically minded and didn't speak much unless the topic was politics. He was well versed on the politics of his country. He understood computers. He spent time showing us its various operations. Leo has visited us since his stay. Whenever he is in the country on business, he visits for Sunday evening dinner. One photo shows him on the floor playing with our grandson Will as a baby. It is good to see him as a mature young man who talks of everything now.

Marta from Spain lived with us as a Rotary student. She was quiet and spent time with other students. She loved the TV show *Friends* and always made sure she saw each weekly episode. She experienced a car wash with Kristin's Scout troop, surprised at another new activity in her life.

Anne from Germany stayed with us for a year. Her parents and sister came for an American Christmas. Anne was an outgoing person with a great smile and loved being with Jay and his friends. She commented, "I like the constant activity of your house." Anne traveled with Kristin and the Girl Scouts to Hilton Head, North Carolina. I was one of the drivers and enjoyed listening to the girls chatter in the car. Anne celebrated her eighteenth birthday on this trip. I was angry with her. "You got a belly button piercing without permission. We're going to the ocean and you could get an infection." I insisted she call her parents and tell them she had this piercing without my permission. They were as angry as I was. I felt vindicated.

Leo from Germany was a thoughtful teen. He knew I loved Ohio State football and bought tickets from a scalper for an enormous price for us to attend a game. "You paid how much?" I asked. I was appalled at the price. We ended up in the opposing team section, but I saw a game! Leo spent most of his time on his phone sitting in the stands calling his friends in Germany and telling them where he was. His parents came for an American Christmas. Our big family seemed to overwhelm them.

Katia, an art teacher from Chile, lived with us for six weeks. She came with a group of teachers from an English speaking school. She attended classes at Ohio State. She and her group of teachers hosted and cooked a farewell dinner at our home for their sponsors. I took them shopping for food. They couldn't find "white powder." I showed them where sugar, flour, and baking powder were shelved. Finally one of them found corn starch, the white powder. The women hand-made menus, served a delicious ethnic meal and showed us dances from their country. Kathy's expertise is Batik. Kathy visited us a few years after her stay and remembered my favorite flower. She had painted a huge iris for me and had it framed. The Batik hangs opposite my kitchen chair where I can see it every day.

Carmen was our last Rotary student. She was from a town in Arequipa, Peru. Bill and I are from Aliquippa, Pennsylvania. We couldn't believe the similarity. She was quiet, but fit into our family. She befriended other exchange girls and spent after school hours with them. She saw her first snow here. Kristin taught her how to make snow angels. Unfortunately, Carmen had to leave the program. She returned to Peru and started at a university.

Our last "exchange student" was from Texas. Elizabeth, a college student to intern in a Columbus company, needed a place to stay. She posted her information on our church bulletin board. Bill and I noticed her request and made arrangements for her to live with us.

Elizabeth and her mother drove to Gahanna in September. Lee and Eileen's second son, our three-month-old grandson David, had been in and out of the hospital since his birth in May with infantile myofibromatosis, a little known serious disease. David passed away the day of their arrival. Elizabeth and her mother were Godsends. They acknowledged our grief and took Bill and me out to dinner that evening. We spent a sorrowful and soul-searching evening with newfound friends who understood death. Elizabeth reported to work the next day and her mother stayed a few days longer than planned. Her calming presence helped us all through new experiences with death.

Elizabeth was a marathon runner. She ran in the Boston marathon. Our family went to Boston to see her run. She had qualified from continuing her days of running in our neighborhood. The marathon was exciting and twice as much to see her run past us and meet her at the end and spend time with her family again. Elizabeth and her father have since visited us. They time their visits to join us for our Sunday evening family dinners.

There are a few things common to all who lived with us. They liked meatloaf, brownies and buckeye candies—typical American foods. The size and availability of our big box stores amazed them. Each student cooked a meal from his/her country before leaving. It surprised me that they all took photographs of our Thanksgiving or Christmas turkeys. The bird wasn't a part of their celebrations. I was proud. They wanted to show my food to their families.

All of us benefited from their stays. It's wonderful to be able to stay in touch through the internet and hear of our global family as adults. I am proud to write that Leo sent me an e-mail: "You have a German grandchild."

Mother of Another

This signature of an exchange student
Fills me with **pride**.
He acknowledges his time with us
and takes in **stride**

That he still feels a part of our family
After many **years.**
He keeps in touch
and brings my **tears.**

I remember him, a teen.
Now with son and wife
From his homeland he corresponds
Successful in professional **life.**

I am grateful to be the mother of another.

TWENTY-THREE

Underneath It All

"This part is mine," said Bill as he knelt on the basement floor on our second day in the Nob Hill House.

"I'm marking my territory."

He was stretching masking tape down the middle of the floor.

"The right side is mine. The left is the kids'."

A stage evolved on the kids' side and a model train layout took shape on their father's side. The masking tape stayed for fifteen years until the kids left home and the entire basement floor became Bill's.

Water caused damage in this basement; not flooding as in the Heil Drive house, but seepage in the walls. An outside pipe cracked and leaking water dampened the walls in the pool table room. Bill and Jay, who was in high school at the time, dug into the nearby ground and replaced the pipe. Inside, they installed new paneling. Two built-in benches were damp and moldy and were removed. The basement has been free from further dampness and flooding. Yet I worry that the Heil Drive flooding nightmare could come back to haunt us.

The children's side filled with toys—a play store and eventually a theatre with two rows of overhead track lights. For backdrops and curtains, the kids hung shower curtain rods from the ceiling draped with bed sheets found at garage sales. Stephen, Kristin, Roy and friends wore dance recital costumes and acted out plays, lip-synced songs from tapes and created plays for the family and neighbors. I was amazed at my children's inventiveness.

They strung scavenged Christmas lights for stage lights and positioned a spot light. For their production of *Little Mermaid*, Roy—then a preschooler who later became our wrestler, Eagle Scout and Marine—wore a bright red jumpsuit and hid until his cue to appear as the crab.

Friends heard about the theatre and contributed items. Candle sticks, strings of pearls, hats and shoes and various pieces of clothing filled my old black college trunk awaiting the kids' next production. I encouraged their interests and was content that my kids liked playing at home. I sat on the steps watching their rehearsals, amazed at their inventiveness.

The family knew Stephen would become an actor, and his ability to "morph" into different characters appeared in each play. I have the memories of driving him all over the city for auditions, rehearsals and appearances in productions. He is a natural on stage. Kristin emerged as a confident person from standing up to her brothers' teasing and in working the light board at Columbus' Children's Theatre. Roy credits his job of turning lights off and on for home productions to his becoming an electrician.

On Bill's side of the basement, train bench construction began within the first month of the move to Nob Hill Court. The track plan designed by Bill on long flights to and from business trips to Japan, became a reality. Bill belongs to a traveling Tuesday night group of model railroaders who come to set up track, scenery, buildings and wiring. Each man has a particular skill. They continue to have fun sharing their hobby. I enjoy listening to their conversations and marvel at their work at creating believable settings.

The trains run on a free standing platform, no water measurements needed along the walls to set up level track as in the Heil Drive house. Trains run in a horseshoe pattern, through the walls into the workshop along the back wall and into the other side of the basement. I left the house when the walls were blasted open for tunnels into the workshop. I didn't want to see my house fall down.

"I need hairspray," Bill said one day.

"Hairspray? You who has a crewcut?" I asked.

"For the railroad," he said. "Sprayed-on puffs of colored fiberglass atop trees, hairspray helps hold the shape of trees full of leaves."

I had to see that! A mountain of trees takes an entire can of spray and appears realistic. Mountains, a steel mill, a formal station, a working turntable and residential area make up other parts of the railroad. A double helix allows trains to climb from one level to another. The industrial area includes miniature warehouses and switching yards. Eight to ten trains run in these sections with men controlling their travels. A tiny video camera mounted in an engine transmitted a video of the area it traveled and sent a signal to a TV where viewers could imagine being the engineer.

❖ ❖ ❖

"There will be a bus in our court Sunday afternoon." This note was sent to the neighbors in our court.

Phone calls followed. "What are you doing now?"

A model railroad convention held in Columbus lined up tours of model railroads in the area and asked Bill to host a visit. Bill's train display brought a busload of thirty people to our basement. "Thirty people in our basement? How will they all fit?"

Bill and I, the engineer and the teacher, devised a plan. The first ten people in the door received a green card which sent them to the basement for ten minutes. The second ten received a red card which sent them to the TV room to view the video from the engines running downstairs. The third ten received a yellow card which led them to the refreshments. At ten minute intervals I rang a bell. "Time to change." Each group moved to another station.

We received compliments on the railroad and the easy flow of people. I watched in awe as the bus driver deftly turned the huge luxury bus around in our court and loaded people for the trip back to Dayton. I walked back into the house proud of my husband and his hobby I'm happy to encourage.

One Sunday morning I heard Bill call from the basement, "Come look at this." I rushed downstairs to see pieces of railroad cars strewn on the workshop floor.

"What happened?" I cried, heartsick to see cracked boxcars lying on their sides, tiny black wheels dotting the floor and animal paw prints on the workbench.

I found Bill looking at a gaping hole above the laundry tub. "An animal got in through the rotting vent from under the deck," he said.

There was a terrific thunderstorm the night before and we guessed the animal ran under our deck and found a way inside. We called the animal exterminator again. He identified the culprit as a raccoon from the footprints left on the tracks and the size of the hole. Bill recovered the entryway and we never saw the critter again. The train cars, now repaired, run on the tracks without raccoon interference.

To the rear of the train room sits a room originally set up as a pool room with overhead lights shining down to the middle of the floor. Our Heil Drive pool table was discarded. With the three older boys out of the house, the pool table was no longer needed for strategy games. The theatre moved into its space. Longer track lights and more rows of curtain rods hung from the ceiling. Our French exchange student, Anne-Laure, painted theatre seats on the wall facing the stage.

Our kids staged a scene from the soundtrack of *Phantom of the Opera*, equipped with an old chandelier strung from the ceiling. One of the neighborhood girls rode her bike over to see the production. When she saw the chandelier tied above the audience seats, she refused to remove her bicycle helmet. I laughed so hard I had to leave the area. The light swung down to the stage at the appropriate time and hit no one!

When the younger ones entered high school, the theatre disappeared and a new pool table filled the center of the room. I stood amazed at the accuracy involved in assembling a pool table. Four men carried three huge, several-hundred-pound slates down the steps and maneuvered around the train display into the back room. The men spent hours stretching and tightening the green baize cover. They tested the balls and their roll and made adjustments for a smooth surface.

I was pleased to see our kids' high school friends come to play pool. I welcomed their friends and hosted many after games, birthday and graduation parties in the garage, TV room, basement and deck. I knew who my kids associated with and enjoyed having them in the house.

The pool room is also a LEGO room. When family pool tournaments end, the old wooden cover is put atop the table for use for LEGO set-ups, a Christmas wrapping paper station and general storage place. I enjoy seeing the grandchildren playing for hours with the millions of LEGOS their fathers and uncles amassed.

The upright freezer moved with us. In the basement, it held sides of beef, frozen fruits and vegetables and frozen cookie dough, and a seemingly never-ending box of frozen "icies," frozen sticks of flavored ice. The ready-to-bake chocolate chip dough rarely made it to the oven. The frozen shapes disappeared from the boxes on the shelves. No one would admit to eating hockey puck shapes and all swore the raw cookies tasted as good as baked ones. As children left home, we needed less and less freezer space and said goodbye to the unit. I was a little sad to see evidence of our former life disappearing. Bill was glad to see the freezer go. Its removal opened more space for the railroad.

One decoration from the previous owners remains. A small bathroom sits under the steps with a sign above the toilet. An optometrist stands to the side pointing to letters as a man is trying to read the one-word chart: "HelpI'mbeingheldprisoner."

"I know something the railroad needs," I said, entering the basement.

"What?" Bill asked, frowning. I know he wondered what I saw lacking in his railroad.

"Black sheets," I said.

He shook his head. "Why?"

I replied, "Hanging from the track to the floor, they will direct the viewer's eye to the trains." He accepted my idea and I discovered how hard it is to find black sheets. The railroad does look professional with boxes and wires hidden underneath the trackage framed in black.

Trains saved our marriage. Spring and summer of 1992 Bill spent three months at home recovering from four eye surgeries for torn retina. We weren't used to being together all day, every day. It was hard to keep the three younger ones quiet and tend to my husband who needed to stay still.

In recuperation, he could not read. Left to right eye movement could re-tear the retina. He could watch TV and work on switchboards for the railroad. Both required steady focus. He spent days in the basement working wiring switches. I spent time in the library, borrowing videos and books. Friends were supportive in taking the kids to swimming lessons, to a movie or into their homes when I needed to drive Bill for surgeries and doctor appointments.

I read to him at bedtimes. The older kids teased us about our "bedtime stories." I read the book *The Oldest Living War Widow Tells All*. We both enjoyed the story and readings with my version of a Southern accent.

That spring we had purchased a new Suburban. Bill could not drive, so I drove Greg to Washington DC on its maiden voyage. We were proud of Greg. As a junior in college, he earned an internship in then Senator John Kasich's office and needed to be in Washington for the summer. I could not let him lose this opportunity, so I took on driving as an adventure. We carefully mapped out our route and Greg and I drove to Washington. I made arrangements to stay with a friend in Virginia after getting Greg settled in a dormitory.

When leaving campus that evening, I took a wrong turn and knew I was lost. I was terrified and said every prayer I knew to calm myself and figure out what to do. My friend had warned me, "Terrible things have happened to women driving alone at night in the DC area. Do not stop if you don't have to." Finally, I saw a parked police car, figured it was safe, and stopped to ask directions. The officer directed me back to the beltway.

Through sheets of rain, I followed a semi trailer's tail lights, again saying all the prayers I knew to get me back safely. My prayers were answered as I began to recognize exits. The semi turned off one exit before mine. I thanked God for him and asked Him to bless the driver on his remaining journey. At 1:00 a.m., I arrived safely at my friend's house. We both had a nightcap as my host was as scared as I was. I was expected three hours earlier. I returned home with a story to tell.

We are not moving from this house. Friends have asked if we would ever leave to live in a condo. Bill says, "The only way I'm leaving is in a pine box." I find that morbid, but I understand him not wanting to rip up years of work on 400 feet of railroad. I want to stay to always have a house big enough to hold our family when they come back for visits. The house is big and flexible enough that if necessary, we could live on one floor.

His Mistress

"It's what's up front that counts," he says.

His mistress lies in darkness
Silently waiting in the basement
Aroused by his arrival
Moves at his command.

He delights in her layout.
Surveys her curves.
Admires her straight legs
Electrifies her.

She fulfills his wishes
Her movements excite him.
She performs beautifully.
Never speaking, always obeying.

Her rhythmic clip
Coupled with low whistles
Alert him to hidden areas
Approaching long stretches.

Slowly, smoothly
Climbing to heights
Controlling descent
He and his mistress rest.

The model railroad run ends.

CHAPTER
TWENTY-FOUR

Front to Back

"Oh no, not again," I cried as I watched rails from the split rail fence drop to the ground.

All six children, when learning to back out of the driveway, veered left and knocked rails out of their posts.

"I didn't mean to," was their cry. In those years, it seemed rails spent more time on the ground than above.

"Sorry," the drivers said, apologizing to the rails.

"Do we need the fence to keep the flowers in?" one quipped, trying a little humor to cover the accident.

Finally, I said, "Dismantle it completely. I don't want to see the ragged rustic rails anymore."

Opposite the now "phantom fence" stands a huge rock. Friends bought a house at the same time we did and their land was dotted with huge rocks. As their house warming present to us, they trucked in a four-foot-high boulder and positioned it at the eastern edge of our drive. The grey boulder continues to sit striped with blue, green and black car paint from cars scraping it backing out of the driveway.

The rock was not always stationary. One of the boys' friends swung wide, hit it with his truck and sent the boulder skidding out in the court. Bill and our boys tied a chain around the rock and attached the end to the trailer hitch of the Suburban. They pulled it back in place as sparks shot out from under it like sparklers on the Fourth of July. Looking at the rock reminds me of the strength of our family and friends—not perfect, but solid.

One July, the front yard was covered in white. It hadn't snowed. Bill and I were away overnight and the teens at home were in charge. The neighbors had discarded oblong strips of foam painted as wooden beams. The fake "beams" had decorated their family room ceiling. Piled at the curb, the foam was irresistible to our boys.

They invited friends to our yard to play "Chicken." Boys rode on each other's shoulders, wielding the foam beams as swords, knocking opponents to the ground. As they made contact, the fake swords exploded into white popcorn-size balls covering the front yard like a snowy January.

I was appalled at the sight of my yard, but glad no one was hurt. I shudder to think what could have happened. We were liable for any injuries. "You could have hurt each other, fallen into the street, not to mention the shouting that bothered the neighbors," I said. "Now clean up this mess."

The boys picked up pieces of foam from my rose bushes, in flower boxes and the "v" of branches of the lilac bush throughout the remainder of the year. They admitted they had nightmares about flying foam. My nightmares were of appearing in front of a judge to explain how someone died on my property.

Our teen drivers had jobs to pay for gas for the cars they drove. Our rule was: "If you keep up your grades, we'll pay car insurance. You pay for gas."

Lee worked in the Gahanna branch of the Columbus Metropolitan Library, Greg at Bob Evans, Jay at Meir's, Stephen at Wendy's, Kristin at Joe's Crab Shack, Roy at Kentucky Fried Chicken and as a "roadie" for a band.

Our garage has held more than cars. One Halloween it was a haunted house. Trick-or-treaters walked through the garage to receive their treat. We heard screams as they walked in the dark into hanging strips of wet crepe paper, screams again as masked friends holding a flashlight on their masks jumped out at people and led them over a small bridge, while a person under the bridge grabbed at their feet. The Halloweeners walked through the garage and out the back door. They followed a path around to the front driveway where I stood dressed as a witch handing out treats.

We heard people saying as they left, "We gotta tell others about this place!"

The next year we could hear people coming up the driveway saying, "Is this the place?"

I'm glad Bill became involved in Halloween. For many years he was late coming home from work on trick-or-treat night. I fed our kids supper, dressed them in costumes, and sent the older boys out, warning them, "Stay together," and then I passed out our treats until Bill came home. The little ones whined because they had to wait for Dad to come home, so I could leave and take them out. Angry and frustrated, I accused Bill, "You're always late on purpose to avoid the household confusion."

"Heavy traffic coming out of the city on Halloween night made me late." By the time he arrived home, I was an angry witch without a costume who stormed out of the house walking the three little ones up and down our street trying to be cheerful.

The haunted garage is gone. Now Bill's "Halloween Hand" scares people. He's retired and home at the start of trick-or-treat night. He sits under an open porch window, and dressed in black, I stand behind him. When I see a Halloweener at the window I nudge Bill and he raises his black gloved hand up and out over the window sill and drops treats into open bags. We hear an astonished "Thank you" as adults standing behind their children stifle giggles. It surprises us that trick-or-treaters come back every year to see "The Hand."

In the back of the garage Bill and the boys built a treehouse around the trunk of a huge tree. It sat directly across from the kitchen window where I could watch the children playing in it. A trap door dropped from the floor, a rope swing and a ladder of boards led to and from the treehouse. I could see kids leaping off the rope into piles of leaves, seated on its floor eating picnic lunches of baloney and cheese sandwiches, swinging stick swords in mock battles and sitting on the railings, dangling their feet quietly looking at the sky.

Seeing the playhouse brought back many friends' memories. "My dad and I built one like that," one visitor commented as he stood for a few long minutes at the kitchen window.

The kids grew too big to play in the tree. Eventually only squirrels scampered there. Boards rotted and fell to the ground. The treehouse disintegrated and all evidence of its happy times were gone. I look at that tree and sometimes can see my children playing up there and hear, "Watch me jump! Come on up! Look how high I climbed!" I miss the children and the treehouse.

When Greg was in a nearby college, he asked to set up a fraternity initiation in our backyard. Pledges were to be led blindfolded in and around our small forest of trees to establish trust in members leading them. I agreed to the exercise thinking it would be harmless. I called each of the families living behind us and warned them. "Big boys will be running around in the yard tomorrow night." Neighbors thanked me for calling and didn't complain.

"You get one cookie when you are done," I told the boys. They frowned, but I continued to tease. I had made Monster Cookies. Peanut butter and M&M dough is dropped on cookie sheets with an ice-cream scoop. Baking cookies spread to hand size with only six to a large cookie sheet. The guys smiled at me when they saw the size. Still, most of the boys ate two! I enjoyed watching them. As they left they called, "Thanks, Mom!" I was pleased to acquire five more sons.

Our deck extends across the back of the house. We enjoy noisy family picnics and celebrations there as well as quiet times sitting reading a book in the sunshine.

"Mom, come look at this!" Stephen called one Christmastime. We had lined the deck banisters with outdoor colored lights. After the first night, none of the lights worked. We stared at bare wires between bulbs. Squirrels had chewed through the cords and blew out the electricity. We laughed, wondering how many fried squirrels we'd find strewn around the yard.

As a preschooler Roy supervised the construction of another's deck. Our neighbors added a large addition and deck to the back of their house. The builder and Roy became buddies. Each day Roy wore his yellow hard hat and took his Tonka trucks over to "help" Bob. He and the builder became good friends. Bob would let Roy and his trucks play on a pile of dirt out of the way and watch the construction. I packed peanut butter and jelly sandwiches for my little builder and he and Bob ate lunch together and talked. I was proud to look out the kitchen window and see my son following orders and working at "his" jobsite. Whenever I see Bob he asks about Roy, and is pleased to know he has become an electrician.

While eating a summer Sunday dinner of pork chops (I remember vividly pork chops) on our deck, fourteen-year-old Stephen received a phone call. He went into the house to answer. When he came back, he said he was no longer needed at the theatre where he was helping young actors. "Did the director give you a reason?" I asked.

"Because I'm gay," Stephen said, and turned and ran off the deck. Bill and I dropped our forks and looked at each other in shock. Speechless, I sat rooted to the chair. I felt a hot knife go through me pinning me to the chair's webbing.

Bill and Greg ran after Stephen. Jay took my hand. "Come with me, Mom," he said, and walked me around the block and let me talk.

"What just happened?" I asked as I stared ahead. "Stephen's going to get beaten up at school. My son could get AIDS and die." I shook my head. "Your brother says he's been bullied on the bus. I didn't believe him. I feel sick. I didn't want to believe it."

Jay said, "Mom, we all knew. There's no problem from us." When we returned I was shaking.

Bill and Greg drove around Gahanna to the home of one of Stephen's friends where they found him and brought him back.

Stephen stood in the doorway hanging his head. "Why did you run?" I asked.

"I thought you'd kick me out of the family."

I reached out and hugged him saying, "Oh, Stephen. We would never do that! You're our son."

I had many questions and fears for my son and we discussed that "Pork Chop Sunday" with him and others throughout the following days. Bill and I sought professional help to "put words around our feelings" and calm our fears.

Stephen said he'd felt different since he was nine. Bill and I could share with him that we'd felt different growing up also. "We were teased about being spoiled only children in a town with large families."

After all our discussions, I have changed my opinion about gay people from disgust to acceptance. I see my son as a happy person with happy friends. I am no longer quick to judge people. I can accept people for who they are and encourage our children to do the same.

Years later, others ran away from our house. One Friday night Roy, thirteen, stayed up late watching a movie and heard noises outside the front of the house. He was on the middle school wrestling team and looked intimidating. He walked around to the front of the house to see classmates tossing rolls of toilet paper up into our trees and over the bushes. Roy stood in the driveway, flexed his muscles and yelled, "What do you think you're doing?"

Two boys ran away and the third one stayed to plead, "We didn't know this was your house. Don't tell your mom. She knows my mom."

Roy said, "I won't tell if you clean this up."

I wasn't sure I believed this story, but our neighbor confirmed it. He was up late studying and saw the whole activity and heard the boys say they wanted to set fire to the toilet paper.

Roy stepped out at the right time. I was extremely upset that boys wanted to "T-paper" and set fire to our house. Also I couldn't believe their bad timing.

After their hasty clean-up, it rained overnight. Wet strips of pink bath tissue hung from trees in the court and stuck to the pavement in our driveway. We cleaned the remaining mess the next morning. A program coordinator was coming to interview our family for hosting an exchange student. We needed to give a good impression as a family who "had it together."

One of the best compliments from raising six Hannas in Gahanna came recently when Kristin and her family were here for a visit. A high school friend arranged to come to the house to see Kristin. Kate entered the kitchen and said, "I didn't know whether to knock or ring the bell, so I just opened the door and called 'hello' and walked in like I always did."

I'm glad people continue to come into our lives and feel welcome in our home. Bill and I have gained brothers and sisters through our friends and learned how brothers and sisters live through our children. When I was a teen, I babysat for a family of five boys. Little did I know that experience would be an omen, and I would live and love in the rooms of a large family as the mom.

Beyond our home, we continued to travel as a family, taking our children to new and exciting places.

He's Driving!

Behind the wheel
Of the family car
Sits
Our beaming sixteen-year-old son
Confident
He'll drive.

Behind the window
Of the family home
Sits
His mother
Confident
She'll worry.

Beside the wheel
Of the family car
Sits
His daring father
Confident
He'll survive.

Behind the wheels
Of the family car
Sits
The reconstructed fence
Confident
It will be hit again.

TWENTY-FIVE

On the Road Again

"What's the Magic number, Mom?"

Summer of 1995 we traveled cross country again by train with Stephen, Kristin and Roy—two teens and a preteen. We built our trip around Bill's business meetings. We boarded in Chicago for Denver, Colorado. We booked a bedroom for Bill and me and one for the three kids. After one night onboard, we heard, "I have no privacy. He kicks all night. It's too hot in there." We knew we had to make a change. We booked another bedroom. The next three nights, the kids took turns sleeping in their special room. Three teens cannot share a train bedroom.

As we traveled upward out of Denver in switchback curves, we could see the back of the train behind us. We'd look down and see the city below us. We were climbing toward six mile Moffat Tunnel, then into Salt Lake City, Utah. We visited the magnificent Mormon Tabernacle and the huge Great Salt Lake. In the train station we learned to make a table of stacked suitcases. We played cards late into the night awaiting a delayed train to California.

As the train traveled the southern route through the Rockies and along the Colorado River, our kids climbed over me to my window of the train car yelling, "Don't look, Mom. People rafting down the river are mooning us!"

In San Francisco, we rented a car and drove to Yosemite National Park. Bill and the kids hiked up the valley for a spectacular view. I lagged behind. I had trouble breathing and frequently had to stop. When I did join them, I was exhausted. We slowly descended. As we left the park, I drove down the two-lane hairpin curves. I gripped the wheel at every turn. "NOBODY TALK," I commanded. "PRAY." Reaching the bottom in silence, I pulled onto the highway. Screams and laughter erupted from the back seat.

"We've been hit." We WERE hit. By feathers! We were following a truck full of live chickens.

We traveled down the West Coast on our way to San Diego. While Bill attended meetings, we toured the San Diego Zoo and the San Diego Navy Port. In planning the trip, we were responsible for the "magic number" of outfits packed in our suitcase. Each of us chose where we wanted to go. Kristin and Roy chose a stay at Disneyland. I chose a tour of Hollywood. Stephen chose a Tommy Tune Broadway-bound musical. Bill's choice was to conclude with a trip to the Grand Canyon.

When we reached Williams, Arizona and the Grand Canyon, we met friends and took the train to the Canyon. On the ride a staged robbery took place. I screamed, "HEY!" as one of the men took my purse.

He returned it later and said, "Lady, I'd like to hire you. You're a good screamer." My kids could have told him that!

On the return trip early one morning outside Kansas City, Kansas, I went to the baggage area on a lower level of the train car. The train had stopped. Two uniformed men with dogs boarded where I was standing. I jumped back, surprised at the visitors. "Ma'am we're checking for drugs," they said. As the dogs sniffed each bag, I asked how they would detect drugs. "People wrap them in dryer sheets to disguise the smell." I gasped and thanked God I did not follow my friend's advice. She told me to avoid wrinkles in packed clothes, fold in dryer sheets.

We flew home from Chicago. I do not like flying! On one trip, Lee sat next to me. When the plane dipped dramatically, I grabbed the armrest between us. I hit the volume button. Lee jumped and threw off his headphones. I almost sent my son through the ceiling. My family tells all, "Don't sit with Mom. It's dangerous."

On our trips back to our hometown to visit my parents, Bill would pack snacks and take the boys to the nearby train yards. Conway, Pennsylvania was a huge switching yard across the Ohio River from Aliquippa. There Bill and the boys would spend all day, watching and taking photos of freight trains arriving, switching cars and departing. Trains were always a part of visits with Grandma and Granddad.

One summer vacation we drove across Pennsylvania with all eight Hannas. We visited the candy factory at Hershey and rode the train through Amish country in Lancaster. In a sepia photo from the train station in Lancaster, we are dressed in Civil War period clothes. Two of the teenage boys stand wearing union uniforms, two wear rebel uniforms. Bill, seated in front of them, wears a railroad engineer's coverall and cap. Five-year-old Roy sits on his knee wearing denim overalls and a neck bandana. Kristin, standing to their left, wears a dress and carries a parasol. Standing to their right, I wear a taffeta gown and a big floppy hat. We were told to pose as we would in "olden times." Males somber. Females, smiling.

"Counting off" in the car assured all Hannas were present. Each called his own number. For long trips we borrowed books on tape. Each child had a small tape recorder to listen to his/her own story. These evolved into CDs and listening to music. We rotated seats to solve the problem of hearing, "Tell him to turn his down. He's breathing on me. I have to go to the bathroom." Bill vividly remembers being in the third seat of our station wagon and the Suburban with his knees at his chin.

The three older boys remember "makeshift TV watching" in the station wagon. With the back seats down and covered with plywood, a space was provided for the boys to lie on their stomachs and watch football. A small black and white TV set was wedged between two front seats and plugged into the cigarette lighter. It received intermittent reception as we traveled through Pennsylvania, West Virginia and Ohio. I smiled as I knew Granddad had encouraged the boys to be Steelers fans. Sunday football games were not to be missed.

In addition to seeing our beautiful country, I hope our kids learned the value of keeping in touch with friends. In our travels, they met people they had heard of from our past or through names signed on Christmas cards. We have a tradition of opening Christmas cards at the dinner table, so all can read cards and hear who has sent us greetings. We talked about who was who. Then, in our travels, the kids could put faces to the names.

Keeping track of all when traveling was a challenge. It was a lesson in planning and cooperation from all of us; from the "magic number" of clothes to pack, activities to do in travel and making alternate plans when needed. As far as we know, we never lost a child on a trip.

Rockies Recorded

Slicing through the silence of the Rockies
Yellow cars behind trailing stream
Round layers of sheared rock.
Unfamiliar scenery
Recorded on passengers' coiled film.

Trainloads of tourists
Gape at hillsides
Higher than their homes
Stare at jutting green mountains
Blocking the sky beyond.

Through open windowed cars
Day's heat adds
Reality to ancestor's travel
As waves of sun's rays
Rise from iron rails.

Flat mesas, towering mountains
Endless cloudless sky
Rhythmic chugging engine
Occasional wild bird cries
Accompany riders through
Colorado's Rockies.

TWENTY-SIX

In All the Rooms

"Twenty-three people in twenty-four hours," I said, reflecting on a past holiday. "Our entire family used every room."

The whole Hanna family came to the Nob Hill Court to celebrate Christmas 2015. Love and laughter filled the rooms and surrounded the house.

Upstairs in the two front bedrooms, Greg and his wife, Nancy, from Chicago and their two children, Ruthie and Evan, slept.

Down the hall, the former boys' bedroom is now the family computer center. Family members flowed in and out throughout the day to send and receive Christmas messages.

Stephen, who lived at home, slept in his bedroom.

In the master suite, Bill and I, Mr. and Mrs. Santa, slept only a few hours and rose early to start coffee and orchestrate the day.

At nine o'clock Christmas morning, the family followed the holiday routine. Lee and Eileen and their boys, Will and Thomas, arrived. Jay, Kristin and Shaun and their three—Olivia, Owen and baby Sam—followed. Roy and Whitney and their children—Gavin, Brooklynn, Rosie and baby Odin—joined the crowd.

Twenty Hannas gathered on the steps for the annual Christmas photo. Greg and Nancy and their two sat at the top, followed by Lee and Eileen and their two teens. Stephen, Kristin and Shaun and their three squeezed on a step below Roy and Whitney, and their four sat on the bottom steps. Bill and I stood on the floor directing the seating and Jay stood upstairs at the railing overlooking the steps taking the picture. We heard again the familiar shouts of, "Move over. He's pushing me. Smile, this may be next year's Christmas card."

After many takes, the family raced to the sunroom shouting, "PRESENTS!" A kaleidoscope of colors of wrapped presents surrounded the tree and train and left little space for all to sit in the room. The men turned around couches in the family room to face the sunroom. Thomas, wearing a Santa hat, played Santa and delivered presents. After a while, we gave up trying to see everyone's gifts.

Adults had drawn two adult names at Thanksgiving. Each person wrote two "wants" on their slip of paper to make gift buying easy. One family draws another family's name for children's presents. Bill and I buy for all grandchildren.

The family room was alive with, "Oohs" and "Aahs" and, "Look what I got!" as people opened presents. Brooklynn and Rosie started drawing designs with their huge collection of colored pens. Toddlers, Sam and Odin, delighted in rolling around in discarded wrapping paper. Ruthie started reading her Nancy Drew book and Olivia began coloring in her adult coloring book. Owen, Gavin and Evan loaded batteries into controls for new remote cars. Watching grandkids excited about their gifts was enough present for me.

After presents were opened, someone yelled, "STOCKINGS" and all ran into the front room in what Bill calls a stampeding herd of turtles.

On the mantel the Christ Child lay in a manger in the family Nativity scene. I'd placed Him in the stable when we came home from Midnight Mass.

Bulging stockings hung like clothes on a wash line under the mantel filled with silly socks, goat milk soaps and tiny flashlights. It's fun to find small presents to suit each person. This year Mrs. Santa gave Kristin and Shaun a tree ornament in the shape of their camper.

With cries of "FOOD," the herd of turtles stampeded into the kitchen for brunch. We hold a food contest at each family gathering with a theme. We have eaten unusual foods—peanut butter soup, chocolate covered bacon and cake on a stick. This Christmas' theme was "Food for Brunch."

Whitney usually wins and this year Shaun was determined to beat her. He served Bloody Marys, drinks decorated with the usual celery stick plus sticks threaded with small foods—meatballs, sausages, shrimp, olives, cherry tomatoes and baby onions and bacon topped with a mini slider! He won.

I was pleased to see the younger generation enter the competition. Olivia created yogurt and fruit cups and Owen assembled "Shirley Temples" for the cousins.

Stephen and Nancy prepared varieties of French toast; Whitney made cheese and sausage roll-ups; Lee made scones and Jay contributed bacon-wrapped shrimp. Greg made omelets, breaking eggs one-handed which he learned from his years as a short-order cook. Shaun's prize was to determine the food for the next contest.

When brunch was over and the kitchen cleaned up by Bill and the men, two men brought up from basement storage one of our wedding presents. They lugged up our fifty-one-year-old electric roaster oven and its stand into the kitchen for cooking the Christmas turkey for dinner. I immediately prepared the twenty-five-pound bird, and placed it in the roaster oven to cook in the afternoon hours. The familiar aroma and anticipation of eating the cooking turkey filled the house as the family played or rested. The Hannas Thanksgiving or Christmas wouldn't be the same without a turkey cooking in the roaster oven.

Outside in the cul-de-sac in front of the house, the children and their fathers tried out presents. The little ones had fun with a "stomp rocket," jumping on a pad that shot off plastic rockets. The older ones took turns shooting darts with a slingshot shooter. One of the hot pink darts stayed high in a neighbor's tree for days until the wind blew it down.

Others drove their remote controlled cars around the court.

Roy and Greg made immediate use of their gifts. Roy received a "pocket hose," a water hose that rolls up into a small space. Greg received rain pants. (He walks home from the train station in all types of Chicago weather.) Greg tried on the rain pants and Roy sprayed him to see if the pants kept him dry.

The demonstration quickly got out of hand and several people who weren't wearing rain pants got wet. Luckily we were the only family in the court at home that day or neighbors would have come out to see those crazy Hannas and their antics.

The younger ones stayed outside and the men went to the basement to shoot pool. Eventually some of the youngsters came inside and were fascinated until dinnertime to watch Grandpap run trains. We could hear their squeals of, "Look what I did! Can I do it again? It's my turn!" when Bill allowed them to operate the log and coal loaders.

At the same time, Owen, Gavin and Evan played basketball outside at the back door of the garage where another present, a mini hoop, was attached. It's still there awaiting their return.

Will and Thomas set the dining room and the kitchen tables for a formal dinner. Ruthie printed place cards and arranged the table seating. In the kitchen, Eileen, Kristin and Whitney prepared the meal while Nancy kept the little ones out of their way in another room. My only job was to cook the turkey and make gravy. I watched others peeling potatoes, baking rolls, and making stuffing. Kristin kept peering over her shoulder saying, "What's the matter, Mom?"

I answered, "I can't believe I'm just sitting in my own kitchen watching, not cooking!"

Again, Bill and the men loaded the dishwasher and cleaned up the kitchen, something they always do when others cook. I am happy to see our sons following their father's tradition.

I've learned the purpose of carrying on traditions. They keep us close, to love and support each other. And now they are being passed down to the next generation.

At the end of a holiday, a Sunday dinner or a birthday celebration, the family knows that the tradition of spending time together anytime will happen again in the many rooms of the Hanna House.

Lost, Hidden or Stolen

It was stolen the moment he arrived.
The phone call left me shaken.
I rushed into the room and gasped.
Others crowded around as wide-eyed as I.
We couldn't believe what we were seeing.
The bundle, unwrapped, laid bare.
Its contents held in the arms of its mother.
My heart was stolen by this tiny creature.
Full of love,
I viewed
my first grandchild
for the first time.

Birthday Boys

Midnight

Newborn grandson
Rests in Grandpap's arms
Perfect present for
Shared birthday.

Grandpap smiles, baby sleeps
Exhausted after his day's journey into the world.
Baby sleeps, Grandpap smiles
Relieved after his day's waiting into night.

Carrying the surname
For future sons
Grandpap, son and grandson pose
Three generations less than an hour old.

Surrounded by two families
Healthy infant boy
Wrapped and capped
Not in hard paper, but soft knits

Becomes the unique birthday gift
For proud Grandpap who
Basking again in the joy of birth
Cradles Gavin, the first child of his last son.

EPILOGUE

Since completing the manuscript for editing, our family has lost another member. Grief had overtaken my will to continue writing about family. I took a year-long hiatus and wrote few revisions.

As previously written, David, our second grandchild, Lee and Eileen's son, died at three months in 2000 from a fatal disease. This past year, 2016, our eleventh grandchild, Rosie, Roy and Whitney's daughter, died at three years old from a tragic (window blind) accident. I grieve for both grandchildren and what could have been. I lost focus. I could not write of family with one so recently missing.

I have come to realize how fragile life is, and through my words hope to portray a strong family who faces trials and tragedies as well as everyday life. In retrospect, this strength propelled me to continue to record our life together and revise sections to give others a clearer view of life in a big family.

After reading my first drafts, the older three commented that they now know their younger brothers and sister better. The younger three commented on now knowing about their brothers' lives before them. As matriarch, I find this heartwarming and continue to write.

Times and I have changed. I have learned some things about myself. My Catholic beliefs have been shaken in my view of gay people and divorce when I see my children adjusting in these worlds and finally being happy. I am more tolerant of others in their situations. I have become more lenient in my thoughts about parenting when I "see the bigger picture," and am not so quick to judge parents' actions when dealing with their children in a technological world. I have come to realize that it's important to reach out and make time to spend with friends. A priest once told me, "Extend an invitation. Let them say no."

Bill and I've made mistakes. We're human.

Recently, at one of our summer Sunday dinners on the deck, amid teasing from table to table I heard, "What? Now you like potato salad? Make sure he gets the veggie burger," and, "Stay seated, Mom. I'll get the napkins." I smiled as I overheard one of our son's friends say, "Your family actually likes each other."

ACKNOWLEDGMENTS

Thank you to my first readers; Carolee Ackinclose, David Bell, Wally Kuhn, Elaine McPeak, Lynn Rumbaugh, the Satellite Group; Frances Bartram, Rose Ann Kalister, Brenda Layman, and Rosalie Ungar; the Ohio Writers' Guild and Sandi Latimer, Columbus Publishing Lab, Brad Pauquette and Emily Hitchcock.

Special thanks to family members who read, commented and added to my story.

Always my love to Bill who helps me continue writing.